SHOELESS SUMMER

The summer of 1923 when
Shoeless Joe Jackson played
baseball in Americus, Georgia

by John Bell

Vabella Publishing

Vabella Publishing
103 Creek Side Drive
Carrollton, Georgia 30116

A portion of the proceeds from the sale of this book will be donated to a childrens' recreation organization.

This book is a factual account based on sources considered to be accurate and reliable and taken in good faith. Any information that is inaccurate or mistaken is completely unintentional. This book is sold with the understanding that the publisher and author are not responsible or liable for inaccuracies from sources considered to be reliable. The publisher and author will not be held responsible or liable for any repercussions or actions stemming from information, accurate or not, learned in this book.

Cover design by Vabella Publishing with special photograph from the Verdo Elmore, Jr. collection.

Manufactured in the United States of America

Library of Congress Cataloging-in-Publication Data
Bell, John, 1969-
   Shoeless summer : summer of 1923 when Shoeless Joe Jackson played
Baseball in Americus, Georgia / by John Bell.
      p. cm.
Includes bibliographical references.
   1.   Jackson, Joe 1888-1951. 2. Baseball players—United
States—Biography. 3. South Georgia League (Baseball league) I. Title.

   GV865.J29 B45 2001
   796.357'092—dc21

                                    2001002912

                   ISBN 0-9712204-0-9

For my son, Jacob

Contents

Author's Notes

Early in the year 2000, I began researching the professional baseball that had been played in Americus, Georgia, my hometown. Growing up about a half mile from the "Green Stadium," I had always heard that Americus had minor league teams that played at the ballpark in years passed. My interest level finally reached the point to where I started compiling information on the professional teams the city had. When I say professional, I mean the teams that were part of an established league with direct ties to major league teams and under the jurisdiction of major league baseball and the commissioner. Americus had teams that fit this description in 1906, 13-15, 35-42, 46-51, and 54.

Americus also had numerous semi-professional teams through the years that belonged to independent leagues over which baseball and the commissioner had no jurisdiction. The 1923 Americus team, which employed "baseball outlaw" Shoeless Joe Jackson, was such a team belonging to the independent South Georgia league. Although a semi-pro team, the historical significance of this team was such that I felt it must be included in the history of Americus professional baseball.

As I sorted out the information pertaining to the 1923 team, I felt that it would not be justified to not tell the whole story from start to finish. It would not be fair to the individuals who put their reputations and livelihoods on the line. It would simply be wrong to cheat the people of today and those of future generations out of knowing the truth about a small town with a passion for our national pastime. I could not in clear conscience only summarize this great story as just another year of many, so I decided to make this a separate work so that all may know the details of the 1923 Americus baseball club and the legendary Shoeless Joe Jackson playing for the team.

I have made every attempt to be as accurate and error-free as possible in this work. If you have questions about any portion of this book, please let me know through letter or e-mail, *belljg@aol.com*. Also, if you have any information to add, again, please contact me. Your thoughts, comments, suggestions, etc. will be most welcome.

Plans are in order for me to complete and publish the history of professional baseball in Americus sometime in the near future. I have been in contact with many of the players who spent time playing in Americus and many of the fans who watched the games. If you have and would like to share any information, photographs, scorecards, stories, etc. about any of the professional baseball teams in Americus, please let me know. Your contribution will be noted and much appreciated.

Thank you very much for reading this book, and I hope you enjoy it.

1923 South Georgia League

1923 South Georgia League

Albany Nut Crackers
Americus (no nickname)
Arlington Bell Ringers
Bainbridge (no nickname)
Blakely Hardwood
Dawson (no nickname)

Introduction

If you know the name Shoeless Joe Jackson, then you are probably already somewhat familiar with the 1919 Chicago "Black Sox" World Series scandal. There are a number of books and movies out that will explain the scandal in great detail including all the participants on and off the field. Just to set the stage, here is a brief and simple recount of how Joe Jackson and seven other members of the 1919 Chicago White Sox baseball team were banned for life from playing organized baseball.

The 1919 team, under the ownership of Charles Comiskey, had a great season winning the pennant and a berth to play the National League champion Cincinnati Reds in the World Series. Comiskey had promised the players bonuses if they, individually, met certain goals and if the team won the American League title, but the Old Roman reneged on his word. News got out that the players were unhappy that they were not getting what they had been promised, and some cheating gamblers decided it was an opportunity to make some easy money. With supposed offerings of large payoffs to certain instrumental White Sox players in exchange for losing the post-season series on purpose, the gamblers had little problem getting "the fix" on.

The eight players who allegedly took money to throw the series are pitcher Eddie Cicotte, pitcher Claude "Lefty" Williams, first baseman Arnold "Chick" Gandil, center fielder Oscar "Happy" Felsch, shortstop Charles "Swede" Risberg, third baseman George "Buck" Weaver, utility player Fred McMullin, and left fielder "Shoeless Joe" Jackson. Buck Weaver and Joe Jackson both vehemently denied taking the dirty money. Jackson's statistics in the World Series were quite indicative that he was not trying to lose on purpose. The White Sox lost the best of nine games series in game eight to Cincinnati, and all eight of these men were tried in a court of law for the conspiracy. Even though Joe Jackson declined the money in exchange for cheating offered to him by one of his teammates, he was brought up along with the rest of the players because of his knowledge of the possible scandal.

In the trial by jury, the eight men were all found innocent of all charges related to the fixing of the 1919 World Series. With total disregard for the court's decision, baseball commissioner Kenesaw Mountain Landis acted on his own and banished all eight men from organized baseball for the rest of their lives.

Shoeless Summer

Summer of 1923, Americus, Georgia

Thursday, May 31, 1923

A meeting was held at the Legion Hall in Americus, Georgia for the purpose of organizing a baseball team to play during the upcoming summer. Approximately seventy-five people were in attendance including members of the Americus Municipal Band, the entertainment for the meeting. Robert C. Lane served as the chairman of the meeting and was one of the featured speakers. Other speakers included Thomas L. Bell, H.P. Everett, Stewart Furlow, A.C. Crockett, and Theron Jennings, all of Americus, and Luther Bloodworth of Macon. Bloodworth was invited to attend to become manager of the team if the organization effort materialized.

Gordon E. Reynolds of Albany sent a telegram to Walter Rylander of Americus that was read at the meeting pledging $50 toward sustaining the Americus team. Reynolds also sent a letter to Rylander noting the enthusiasm of the cities of Dawson, Arlington, and Albany to have teams organized. Another telegram from Cliff Pantone was read offering to bring the heart of the University of Georgia baseball team to fill the Americus uniforms if the organization effort was perfected.

After the hearing of the letter and telegrams, it was decided that funds would be solicited from the people of Americus to support the baseball club organization effort. If enough financial support could be shown in this initial solicitation, it was believed that the same support would be present throughout the summer. A committee to oversee the fund raising was named which included Robert C. Lane, Thomas L. Bell, H.P. Everett, Stewart Furlow, A.C. Crockett, Theron Jennings, Dan Chappell, Sam R. Heys, Bradley Hogg, Nathan Murray, and Alton Codgell. Crockett was selected to serve temporarily as the secretary of the proposed baseball club.

Friday, June 1, 1923

The solicitation committee announced that they would begin to collect funds for the organization of the Americus baseball team on Monday, June 4. "It is hoped that those interested in this movement will have determined by that time just what amount they will give to support a real winning baseball team," R.C. Lane and Theron Jennings were quoted as saying. Jennings continued by saying, "It is not the idea of the committee that anyone is to be asked to sign pledges, or in any way obligate themselves to donate further to the team. If we are to

3

procure the necessary out-of-town players to produce a winning club, we must give this money to the committee, headed by A.C. Crockett, temporary secretary and treasurer, next Monday. Mr. Luther Bloodworth has contracts pending with several college players who must know where they are to play ball this summer not later than Monday, and the proposed manager must be notified at that time whether or not Americus will support a ball team."

The committee wanted to make it clear that as players from out-of-town were going to be offered positions on the team, the same opportunity would be afforded to every local player who could play the class of baseball necessary to win games.

A great deal of encouragement was given the committee from the Americus citizens who had heard of the upcoming solicitation. It was the general opinion that the necessary funds would be raised with little or no trouble.

Monday, June 4, 1923

R.C. Lane reported that the committee soliciting funds to support the Americus baseball team for the summer raised $550. This was only about half of the sum agreed upon needed to support the team. Superior court being in session was blamed for the shortness of funds being raised as a number of attorneys and other baseball enthusiasts were unavailable to make donations. Hundreds of citizens praised the committee's efforts and promised consistent attendance at the games throughout the summer. Fund raising would continue until finished, and an announcement pertaining to the organization of the team would follow.

Baseball fans from Albany made it known that they wanted to see the Americus team materialize, as the two cities were old sports rivals. Games between the two teams were believed to draw attendance in record numbers. Funds were already raised to support teams in Albany, Dawson, and Arlington for the summer, and these three wanted to see Americus as a fourth city in their baseball playing area. They did not want to have an organized league or to play each other exclusively. Americus was simply needed to have an even number of teams in the immediate vicinity to give assurance of always having a game to play.

Saturday, June 9, 1923

With collections ongoing for the Americus baseball club, it was reported that the campaign committee had now raised approximately $1,000 with their goal now being $1,500. Gordon Reynolds of Albany came to Americus with news that five clubs are now going to make up the area loop, Blakely and Bainbridge now showing interest, and Americus must come in to be the sixth. He also guaranteed that the first game of the season would be played in Americus against Albany. With six teams a strong possibility, thoughts were turning to forming a league of the six and playing among each other exclusively. Reynolds and Sid Stern of Albany spent the day in Americus with the committee hyping the proposed baseball team. "Americus is a good baseball town and with a team composed of good, clean college fellows, I believe the team will be self-supporting," Reynolds said. Reynolds even donated $50 from his own pocket to move the Americus baseball effort forward.

The Americus Times-Recorder newspaper joined in the promotion of the team by saying "An afternoon on the bleachers will get the kinks out of your brain, and you'll feel better on the morrow." The paper went on to say "The Times-Recorder does not say that no town is a progressive town until it has a baseball team, but it does say that most progressive towns have baseball."

Monday, June 11, 1923

The fund-raising total had reached $1,100, and Americus was promised a "fast amateur baseball team" for the summer by newly appointed club field manager Bradley Hogg. Hogg, a member of the fund raising committee, won the job over the previously considered candidate, Luther Bloodworth. A meeting was schedule for this night to decide the rest of the officials for the team, and all who had given money to the organization effort were urged to attend. Americus was now going to be the sixth team of the newly organized South Georgia league of semi-professional baseball. The other cities on the circuit would be Albany, Arlington, Bainbridge, Blakely, and Dawson. Exhibition games were already schedule to be played between Albany, Arlington, Bainbridge, and Dawson beginning on Wednesday, June 13. The regular season playing schedule between all the teams of the new league would be announced within the next ten days.

Once Hogg got the reigns of the Americus team, he had several contracts pending with players including Luther Bloodworth, formerly of Mercer University, to pitch for the team. Negotiations were also in progress with James "Skinny" Hines of Sumter County; Bill Parsons who had formerly worn a Souther Field uniform; Bob Lane who was instrumental in organizing the team; Edwin Player, a former Americus High School baseball standout; Darby Reid, another high school player; and Buddy Barefield. Practice among these players was to begin immediately at the Playground diamond next to the Americus city swimming pool at Hill Street and Barlow, the home field of the Americus team. Fans were encouraged to attend practices to encourage those athletes trying for positions on what was sure to be a fast team.

1923 South Georgia League

Map showing the 1923 South Georgia League cities

Tuesday, June 12, 1923

Albany and Dawson both announced their rosters for the baseball season. Albany's initial lineup consisted of pitchers Jack Slappey of Albany, Chick Eady of Savannah, Happy Bell of Jacksonville, Florida, T.R. Brown of Barnwell, South Carolina, catchers Bill Kimbrell of Albany, Louis Angel of Franklin, North Carolina, first baseman Tot McCollough of Nashville, Tennessee, second baseman Cliff Cameron of Albany, shortstop Guy Rogers of Atlanta, third baseman Elliott Cooper of Columbus, left fielder Harry Eldridge of the University of Georgia, center fielder Sam Boney of the University of Georgia, right fielder Pop Ramsey of the University of Georgia, and utility player Duck Swann of Macon. No manager was appointed, but Gordon Reynolds would act as manager until the players arrived. Reynolds would then appoint a player-manager from the squad.

Dawson's lineup was announced to be composed of pitchers Emmett Hines of Georgia Tech, Minchew of Moultrie, Hap Henderson of Dawson, catcher Eddie Rawson, first baseman Lightfoot, second baseman Pinkston, shortstops Brogdon, Mannion, third baseman Raefle, outfielders Daniel, Poore, and Sullivan.

Wednesday, June 13, 1923

Blakely announced that Wallace Wade had been hired to build their baseball team, and he would stay on serving as manager of the club. Wade spent the previous year in the role of baseball coach at Vanderbilt University. He was also contracted to fill the head coach's job at the University of Alabama for the upcoming year.

Pre-season play began today between Bainbridge and Dawson with Bainbridge coming out ahead, 4 to 1. Games were scheduled for the next ten days for these two clubs and for Albany and Arlington. If Americus and Blakely could get their teams together before the start of the regular season, it was decided that they could play each other in exhibition play if they wished. The first official games of the season were tentatively scheduled for Monday, June 25.

Thursday, June 14, 1923

Pre-season action continued as Albany and Arlington tied 4 to 4 in a game played in Albany. Dawson settled the loss from the day before by defeating Bainbridge 5 to 2 in Dawson.

Friday, June 15, 1923

Americus field manager Bradley Hogg announced that sixteen men had been invited to practice that afternoon. Tentatively signed to play for Americus were pitchers Morris Overstreet of Hahira, Jack Holland of Bronwood, James "Skinny" Hines of Americus, second baseman Bill Cox formerly of Olglethorpe University, shortstop Harvey Weatherby of Atlanta, third baseman Boswell, outfielder Eddie Wade of Parrott, and catchers Aney Walker of Griffin, and Pony Cox of Howard College in Birmingham, Alabama. Several local players being given tryouts on the team were Edwin Player, Bill Parsons, Kinson Finley, and Shirah of Plains. These players were considered to be strong prospects to give Americus a winning baseball club in the South Georgia league.

Arlington played host to Albany and lost 6 to 2 in exhibition action. More than 1,500 fans packed the stands to see Albany pitcher Wally Norris defeat Arlington's Tige Stone.

Monday, June 18, 1923

Dawson handed Albany a pre-season loss by winning 9 to 6. Dawson took the lead in the first inning and never looked back. Albany hitters Henderson, Daniels, and Kimbrell each hit long balls the Dawson yard could not hold, but these were not enough to turn the tide.

Tuesday, June 19, 1923

Pre-season games continued as Bainbridge's Red Moseley held Arlington to a shut out until the bottom of the ninth inning when Arlington struck for two runs. The last minute rally was exciting but not enough to take the lead over Bainbridge. Tige Stone took the loss for Arlington with the final score being 3 to 2. Stone's pitching was excellent, but errors caused all three runs and cost him the game.

Dawson shutout Albany 3 to 0 at the Albany ball field. Dawson pitcher Sullivan gave up only two hits in the contest while Wally Norris, pitching for Albany, was hit quite freely.

Wednesday, June 20, 1923

A committee of Americus baseball enthusiasts visited Albany for the task of arranging the opening game of the regular season in the South Georgia circuit. The committee was made up of W.W. Ray, Thomas L. Bell, Rufus Lane, and Alton Cogdell. Upon their return, they were to announce the opening date for the promised contest between Americus and Albany.

The fence committee, which was assembled on Tuesday, June 19 to solicit funds to erect a fence around the outfield of the Americus Playground ball field, had tremendous success in their fund raising efforts. They had only two citizens decline to make a donation of $1 to their cause.

Albany upset Dawson in a ninth inning rally scoring four runs to beat the home team 7 to 4. Bainbridge, playing host to Arlington, lost 3 to 2.

Thursday, June 21, 1923

The announcement came from Rufus Lane that Americus would open its baseball season by hosting the Albany Nut Crackers on Monday, June 25. This decision was made when a baseball committee from Americus visited Albany the day before. Along with the Americus coalition were Dan Gibson of Albany, R.H. "Bob" Bostwick of Arlington, W.W. Smith of Blakely, Mr. Stackhouse of Bainbridge, and Mr. Cox of Dawson. The league's organization was made official at this meeting by the election of Mr. Stackhouse to serve as the league president and Dan Gibson to serve as secretary-treasurer. A board of directors for the league was also chosen to be Stackhouse, Gibson, Lane, Bostwick, Cox, and Smith.

Representatives from the cities of Moultrie, Colquitt, and Quincy, Florida came to the meeting each hoping to have their city included in the league instead of Americus. Albany officials, entertaining the idea of one of the other cities present filling the sixth slot, asked Americus when the team would be ready to play. "Americus is ready to play today; all we are waiting on is a team to play with," the Americus officials boasted to keep their place in the circuit secured. The business of putting together the season schedule began after this statement solidified Americus as the sixth and final team in the South Georgia league.

The South Georgia baseball season would start on Monday, June 25 and run for the next eight weeks the league directors decided. There would be two halves to the season, four weeks each, with the team having the best record in each half playing each other for the league championship at the end of the season. Games would be played Monday through Saturday, and Sundays would be off days.

The Americus team played its first game in the form of an exhibition contest against an outside the league team from Montezuma, Georgia. Approximately two hundred, seventy-five fans came out to the Playground diamond to see Americus win by a final of 8 to 1. Red Laird went the distance on the mound for Americus and struck out nine of the visiting batters. Laird also added to his cause with a home run in the bottom of the fifth. The Americus lineup consisted of Rogers at shortstop, Cox at second, Brewer at first, Brown in left field, Parsons in right, Lane in center, Shirah at third, Pony Cox behind the plate, and Laird pitching. Shirah was being given a tryout for the team in this game, and he was the only Americus player who did not get on base. The fans of Americus were impressed with the good showing in the first ever game played by the team.

In other pre-season baseball, Arlington beat Dawson 5 to 4 in ten innings at the Arlington field. The game was filled with exciting plays and capped off by Ike Thrasher's single with two men on to drive in the winning Arlington run. Bainbridge was defeated on their home grounds by Albany, 6 to 4. Albany's big inning was the third when all six of their runs were scored.

9

Ad that appeared in the June 22, 1923 edition of the Americus Times-Recorder

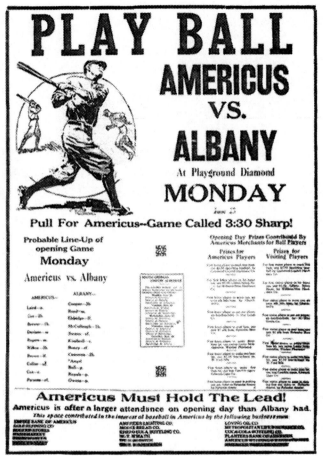

Ad that appeared in the June 22, 1923 edition of the Americus Times-Recorder

Friday, June 22, 1923

The fence fund was reported to be nearing the goal of $150 that was needed to put a fence around the outfield of the Playground diamond. Being only four dollars short, construction of the fence would begin immediately with confidence that the remainder would be raised by the time of completion.

Americus played the second game of the team's history against the same Montezuma team as the day before. In this game, Americus took its first loss by a close score of 3 to 2 on the Montezuma home field. "Big Bill" Parsons took the loss doing the pitching for Americus while Montezuma's Anderson pitched for the win. Americus made an effort in the seventh, but it was quickly snuffed out by the Montezuma defense.

The Dawson team beat Arlington in Dawson 10 runs to 4. Pitcher Sullivan got the win for Dawson in a game that was plagued with errors. Albany used three pitchers in a home game against Bainbridge but still lost by a score of 10 to 4.

Saturday, June 23, 1923

Americus traveled to Blakely for the team's first game against another South Georgia league team. It was decided by the league officials that these two teams could play each other in exhibition play if they got their teams ready before the start of the season. Albany, Arlington, Bainbridge, and Dawson had already been playing pre-season games with each other since June 13. The game was fast and well played between Americus and the Hardwood bunch and ended in a 4 to 4 tie.

Monday, June 25, 1923

The opening game of the regular season was played at the Playground as Americus hosted Albany in a tie 3 to 3 game. Approximately six hundred fans, half Albany and half Americus, turned out to see the game that ended in the eighth inning due to rain. Red Laird pitched beautifully for Americus giving up three runs on two hits and striking out eight. Catcher Jimmie Clements hit a home run, center fielder Jasper Parker got a double, and first baseman Paul Collier went two for three for the home team. Chick Eady also pitched excellent ball for the Nut Crackers allowing three runs on six hits, two walks, and three strikeouts. Rain began to fall as Americus scored the tying run in the bottom of the seventh. As Albany came to bat in the top of the eighth, the rain really came down, and the game was called.

All five other teams in the South Georgia league began the season with a public subscription of funds of $3,000 or more while Americus had only raised about $1,200. Moultrie and Quincy, Florida also had over $3,000 in hand when Americus was awarded the last franchise in the league over both of them. An article appeared in the Americus Times-Recorder offering fans subscriptions to the baseball guarantee fund for $5 per month for two months to cover the season. With the subscription came a season pass to all home games. Gate receipts would not cover the expenses of the team, so the team officials were seeking to sell one hundred subscriptions. Nineteen subscriptions had already been sold, and ladies could purchase a season pass $1 per month with a grandstand pass being 25 cents more.

The Arlington team, which had come to be known as "Uncle Bob Bostwick's Bell Ringers," upset Bainbridge on their home field by a score of 6 to 4. Bainbridge pitcher Yank Roberts ended a fifteen scoreless inning streak from the pre-season taking the loss in this contest. This game was the only win to be had in the circuit, as Dawson at Blakely was a rainout.

Tuesday, June 26, 1923

The scheduled game of Americus at Bainbridge was cancelled due to rain. Jupiter Pluvius also caused the cancellation of Blakely hosting Dawson. Arlington's "Bell Ringers" were shutout by Albany 5 to 0 in the only game played in the South Georgia circuit. "Shaky" Kain, pitching for Albany, got the win and much support from utility man Duck Swann who hit one over the fence and made a key, spectacular catch in center field. Luther Bloodworth, who earlier was considered for the Americus field manager job then offered a position on the pitching staff, took the loss for Arlington.

Wednesday, June 27, 1923

Approximately four hundred, sixty-five fans witnessed Americus lose to Bainbridge at the Playground diamond by a score of 4 to 1. Americus pitcher, Otis Bassinger, who manager Bradley Hogg recruited from Texas, got the loss in the contest. The left-hander allowed seven hits and issued two walks, but he also struck out six, which was pleasing to the home fans. Errors plagued Americus as the team accumulated twelve total, nine of which came from catcher Pony Cox. The highlight of the game was a rollover catch made by Americus third sacker Gid Wilkes in the second inning. Red Brown and Cliff Pantone each got a two-base hit and went two for four on the day. Paul Collier also batted .500 with two hits in four trips in the game.

Albany beat Arlington for the second time in as many games 5 to 4 in Arlington. Albany mound artist Jack Slappey struck out fifteen batsmen accounting for over half of the put outs by the defense. Jack Holland was on the mound for Arlington until the seventh when he was relieved by Luther Bloodworth. All of the Albany runs were allowed by Holland.

Dawson defeated Blakely 4 to 3 in what was called one of the best games ever played in Dawson's Baldwin Park. Dawson took the lead in the bottom of the eighth inning and held on through Blakely's turn at bat in the ninth.

Thursday, June 28, 1923

In the only game the rain allowed to be played, Americus took a clobbering from the visiting Dawson team on the very muddy Playground diamond. The final score was 14 to 6 as Americus used four different pitchers in the game including manager Bradley Hogg. Morris Overstreet was pitching quite ineffectively for Americus and was relieved in the second inning by Lefty Owens. Owens retired the only batter he faced but had to leave the game in the next inning after being hit by a pitch. Manager Hogg came on to pitch in the third, but soon found that he couldn't get the Dawson hitters under control. He called "Big Bill" Parsons in from right field to hurl the rest of the game and brought Edwin Player off the bench to take right. Pony Cox, the catcher for Americus, allowed five passed balls on the day, which only worsened the already distressed pitching. The highlight of the game for Americus was a circus catch by Red Laird in center field that was said to be worth the price of admission. Edwin Player and Bill Parsons both were two for three on the day, and Red Brown got two hits in five at bats. Pony Cox got a double on his only hit, and Hub Dowis, Pinkston, and Paul Collier turned a beautiful six-four-three double play. Former Georgia Tech star Emmett Hines was on the hill for Dawson pitching steadily throughout the wet game. Dawson made quite a showing in their first appearance at the Playground.

Friday, June 29, 1923

The Americus baseball officials arranged for a section of the Playground diamond for black baseball fans to be seated. "The action was taken by the directors after a discussion in which the support given the team by Americus Negroes already was heartily praised," the article in the Americus Times-Recorder read. It was pointed out that the section would be protected from foul balls by the same wire screen that protected the rest of the seats. There would not be overhead covering in this section, but many of the seats in the park were not covered.

Americus traveled to Dawson for the third game of the three game set and prevented the sweep winning 8 to 3. Red Laird pitched nine strong innings and got good run support from the rest of the team in the first win of the official season for Americus. Laird surrendered three runs on six hits, three walks, and three strikeouts. Catcher Barnhart and center fielder Red Brown led the offense for Americus with three and two hits respectively in five at bats each. Minchew, on the mound for Dawson, took the team's first loss of the young season.

Blakely got a home field win from Arlington, 5 to 2, as Goat Cochran pitched in his usual good form for the win. Both of Arlington's runs were caused by errors in the ninth inning. Albany maintained an undefeated record by taking two games from Bainbridge. The scores were 5 to 3 and 2 to 0 in the double-header played at the Nut Cracker home field.

Saturday, June 30, 1923

Even though Americus lost a heart breaker of a game 11 to 10, the fans called it the best game seen thus far in the 1923 season. It took thirteen innings for Dawson to finally beat Americus at the Playground ball yard. The winning run came when Americus catcher Barnhart dropped the ball allowing Dawson shortstop Cosby to score on a play that should have been an easy out. Offensively, Paul Collier went two for seven with a double, Bill Parsons was good twice in six trips with a two-bagger, and Dumas got a double and a triple for his two hits in six at bats. Center fielder Spikes was two for seven, catcher Barnhart was two for five, and second baseman Pinkston was three out of seven in hits. Otis Bassinger, Morris Overstreet, and Red Laird each pitched for Americus with Laird taking the loss. Sullivan got the win for the visiting Dawson team.

Other South Georgia league games saw the Hardwood gang of Blakely narrowly defeat Arlington 6 to 5 at Arlington. Bainbridge ended Albany's four game winning streak and blemished their undefeated record in a fast game at Bainbridge 6 to 1.

At the end of the first week of the South Georgia circuit's season, Albany was in first place with a four and one record. Dawson was a half game in second with a record of three and one. Blakely held third place with two wins and one loss, one full game out of first. Bainbridge had the fourth slot two games out of first with a two and three record. Americus had one win and three losses with a two and a half game margin between them and Albany for fifth place. Uncle Bob's gang from Arlington brought up the rear with one win and four losses, three full game back.

Monday, July 2, 1923

Americus visited Albany for the first time in the season and was welcomed with a 6 to 2 loss. Albany took the lead in the third inning and kept it until the last Americus batsman went down. Lefty Owens

15

pitched fairly well for Americus and giving up eight hits, walking one, and striking out four, but errors by Collier, Dumas, and Pinkston allowed vital runs to score for Albany. Third baseman Hub Dowis hit a double for Americus going two for three on the day. Dumas was two for four, both singles, and Bill Parsons was batted 1.000 going two for two. Albany pitcher Greene Farrer got the win for the visiting team allowing two runs on seven hits, four walks, and six strikeouts.

Bainbridge was victorious over Blakely by a score of 5 to 3 in a fast game at the Bainbridge diamond. Al Cordell was the winning pitcher for Bainbridge while Blakely's Morris took the loss. Dawson won at home against Arlington in a high scoring game that ended at 11 to 7.

Tuesday, July 3, 1923

In a fast game kept cool by light rain throughout, Americus beat Albany 5 to 4 at the Playground diamond. Albany struck first in the game for two runs in the top of the third inning. Americus answered with five runs in the bottom half of the inning, and this was all the home team needed to secure the win. Red Laird pitched good baseball for nine innings striking out two and walking two to get the win while Albany's Chick Eady took the loss with five strikeouts and four free passes. Offensive highlights for Americus were a double by catcher Barnhart for his only hit in five trips to the plate and a triple by shortstop Dumas going two for two. Red Brown was also two out of two, both singles. In the field, Americus turned two double plays during the game, four-six-three and three-six-three. Albany first baseman Tot McCullough went four for four with one double.

The other two games in the South Georgia circuit were also won by only one run. Blakely hosted Bainbridge and won 6 to 5. Dawson lost to Arlington at Baldwin Park in Dawson by the narrow margin of 8 to 7.

Wednesday, July 4, 1923

In celebration of our nation's one hundred, forty-seventh birthday, the teams of the South Georgia league decided that each city should have a home field contest of our national pastime. This meant a double header for everybody as well as a road trip in the heat of the day.

Americus and Albany were paired up to play two with the morning game being scheduled at the Playground diamond and the afternoon game in Albany. In the morning contest, approximately one thousand fans witnessed Americus lose to Albany 4 to 1 with Otis Bassinger taking the loss on eight hits, one walk, and four strikeouts. Cliff Camp got the win for the Nut Crackers allowing Americus batters only two hits in the entire game and striking out three. The afternoon game in Albany proved to be an exciting one as more than two thousand patrons turned out to watch. With a 5 to 5 tie going into the bottom of the ninth, Albany first baseman Tot McCullough came to bat with two on and two out. After two balls, newly acquired Savannah city league pitcher Paul delivered one down the middle that was met by McCullough's bat sending the ball over the right-center field fence. Albany won the game 8 to 5 in exciting fashion making it two wins on the day over Americus. Shaky Kain was the winning pitcher of the game allowing five runs on eight hits. Eddie Wade hit a homer for Americus going two for five, and Dowis, Dumas, Collier, and Barnhart each hit a double. Barnhart also got a single for his other hit in five trips to the plate.

Game one of the day between Arlington and Dawson resulted in a win for Arlington at the Dawson baseball field. Arlington pitcher Will Koenigemark got the win for the Bell Ringers, and Dawson pitcher Hap Henderson got the loss in the 4 to 3 morning game. In the afternoon game at Arlington, it was Dawson getting revenge with a final score of 11 to 8. Hap Henderson got the loss in this one too pitching the first part of the game then being relieved by Sullivan. Wally Norris got the win for Uncle Bob's team in this high scoring game that saw home runs hit by Dawson's Daniels and Mannion and Arlington's Davis.

Blakely and Bainbridge split their games played on Independence Day. The morning game was won by Bainbridge on the Blakely diamond 6 to 5. Dowis was the winning pitcher with help from Yank Roberts while Morris took the loss relieving Liles and Wade on the Blakely pitching staff. The afternoon contest was another close game, but Blakely came out on the winning side in this one. With the final score of 4 to 3, Goat Cochran got the win for Blakely and Hecker took the loss for Bainbridge.

At the end of the July 4th games, it was Albany at the top of the standings followed in order by Blakely, Dawson, Bainbridge and Arlington tied for fourth, and Americus bringing up the rear.

Thursday, July 5, 1923

Tragedy struck the family of Americus infielder Hub Dowis as he learned of the death of his brother O.B. Dowis. It was called an assassination, as Hub's brother had been a deputy sheriff in Duluth,

Georgia where the murder took place. Hub left Americus after receiving this news to travel to Duluth. He was expected to return after a few days, but he would never rejoin the team.

Bradley Hogg resigned his position as field manager of the Americus baseball team. Hogg's record of three wins, six losses, and one tie on the less than two-week old season had Americus in last place in the six-team South Georgia circuit. Thomas L. Bell, one of the founders of the team, was asked to serve as interim manager with full support pledged behind him by the directors of the Americus Baseball association as well as the fans present at the meeting. Plans were made to raise a fund of $500 a month, the amount that was necessary to support the team's payroll and other expenses. Tom Bell was no stranger to running a ball club as he had managed semi-pro baseball in Americus several years prior. Bell promised that if the fans wanted good baseball and were willing to put up the cash to pay for it, then he would give the city a first-class team.

Action on the Playground diamond saw Americus narrowly beat Blakely by a score of 3 to 2. It should have been a shut out game with Lefty Owens on the mound for Americus, but two errors from center fielder Eddie Wade and one from shortstop Dumas allowed two Blakely runs to score in the top of the sixth. A squabble also arose during this inning when there was a misunderstanding of the Americus Playground ground rules. Blakely had the bases loaded when second baseman Neil singled to short. The ball was overthrown and got stuck in the bleacher wire and became a "dead ball." The ground rule was to allow each base runner the base he was nearing and one additional base after the ball became dead. This should have put the batter at third, scored all three base runners, and tied the game at three, but Umpire Sergeant Stewart ruled differently. Not familiar with the local ground rules, Stewart ruled the batter back to second base and the man who was on first back to third. Heated arguments arose and confusion took over until Blakely manager Wallace Wade entered a formal protest of the game and a statement of the Americus ground rules was signed by Wade, Americus manager Tom Bell, and Umpire Stewart. The protest would be forwarded to the circuit secretary N.P. Cornish of Savannah, former president of the Sally League, for ruling. Owens got credit for the win allowing five hits, two walks, and striking out two. Blakely's Laing took the loss allowing seven hits, no walks, and issuing two strikeouts. Hub Dowis and Bill Parsons each got a double, Paul Collier went two for four, and Barnhart had two singles in two at bats. Dumas and Eddie Wade each had a stolen base in the game.

Dawson hosted Albany and was defeated by the visiting team 9 to 1. Greene Farrar got the easy win for Albany, and Morris

Overstreet, formerly with Americus, took the loss on the Dawson side. Tot McCullough was the offensive star of the game for Albany with a double and a home run. Arlington shutout Bainbridge, 3 to 0, in the third game of the day in the South Georgia circuit. Tige Stone was in his old form getting the win for Arlington and allowing only two hits on his home field. Al Cordell took the loss for Bainbridge pitching well but not getting the necessary offensive support from his team.

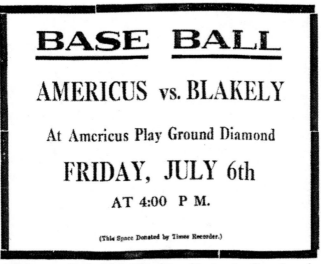

BASE BALL

AMERICUS vs. BLAKELY

At Americus Play Ground Diamond

FRIDAY, JULY 6th

AT 4:00 P M.

(This Space Donated by Times Recorder.)

Ad that appeared in the July 5, 1923 edition of the Americus Times-Recorder

Friday, July 6, 1923

With a new manager Tom Bell at the helm for his second game, the Americus squad won against Blakely, 3 to 2, in an exciting tenth inning rally on the Playground diamond. With the absence of Hub Dowis at third, Gid Wilkes stepped in to take the position. After Blakely took a 2 to 1 lead in the top of the tenth, it was Wilkes leading off in the bottom of the inning. Unable to connect with the offerings of Blakely pitcher Morris, Wilkes reached first when catcher Fincher dropped the third strike. Fincher threw wild to first on the play allowing Wilkes to make it safely to second. Dumas followed with a single, moving Wilkes to third, and stole second. Barnhart beat out a bunt as the next Americus batsman loading the bases. Paul "Big Boy"

Collier drew a walk as the next man up pushing Wilkes across the plate to tie the game. Paul grounded to third forcing Dumas out at home. With the bases still loaded, Red Brown found a gap at third scoring Barnhart to win the game for the home team. Red Laird got the win for Americus striking out six Blakely batters, walking three, and giving up seven hits in ten innings of work. Dumas got a double in the game going two out of four, Barnhart was two for three, and Collier was safe three out of four times at bat. The Americus infield turned a beautiful four-six-three double play in the game.

Other action in the South Georgia league saw Arlington beat Bainbridge, 5 to 1, in Arlington. Dawson hosted Albany and defeated them by a 7 to 5 final score.

Saturday, July 7, 1923

Americus field manager Tom Bell signed Howard Wright of Eastman to play catcher for the club in an effort to strengthen the team and spark the other players to win more games. Wright was called the best catcher in the state of Georgia at the time. His excellent bat and arm along with his strong personality were planned to bring a pennant for the Americus team. Barnhart, who had been doing well behind the plate in every game since he came to the team, would be moved to a more accustomed position in the outfield.

In the team's first official appearance at the Blakely diamond, Americus defeated the Hardwood team 7 to 3. Otis Bassinger took the win for Americus allowing six hits, issuing two walks, and striking out four while Blakely pitcher Goat Cochran got the loss. Americus won on a nine hits and five walks which manufactured seven runs. Eddie Wade and Barnhart both went two for four on the day for Americus taking the top batting honors.

Dawson defeated Albany in a high scoring game in Albany, 12 to 8. Arlington and Bainbridge also had many tallies in a contest at Bainbridge where the score was 13 to 6 in favor of Arlington.

At the end of the second full week of the South Georgia league, Albany held first place with eight wins and four losses. Arlington was one game behind with a seven and five record. Dawson was in third place by a game and a half at six and five. In fourth place was Americus, two and a half games out of first, with a record of five and six. Blakely was in fifth place, a half game behind Americus, with four wins and six losses. Bainbridge brought up the rear of the league with a four and eight record and four games behind first. Americus and Blakely could have their records adjusted depending on the ruling of the protested July 5 game.

Sunday, July 8, 1923

Players from the Americus baseball team were guests at a supper at the Windsor Hotel in Americus given by several fans of the team in congratulations for a three game winning streak. Present at the celebration were Barnhart, Wright, Collier, Dumas, Wilkes, Brown, Parsons, Paul, and Bassinger. Manager Tom Bell and Team Director Rufus Lane were present as chaperones of the dinner. Another social gathering for the team was planned in the form of a "melon cutting" for Monday night at the home of Tom Bell.

Monday, July 9, 1923

The three game winning streak was broken at the slippery Playground ball yard as Americus was shut out by Arlington 3 to 0. Paul, on the mound for Americus, pitched effectively, but errors prevailed through the seven innings played before darkness overtook the game. Five errors combined by all four Americus infielders allowed Arlington to score two runs in the fourth and one more in the fifth. The Americus bats were active with eight hits off Arlington hurler Tige Stone, but the hits were so scattered that no tallies were gained. Paul allowed five hits, three walks, and issued three strikeouts. Eddie Wade hit two doubles with a three for four record on the day, and Paul Collier got one as his only hit in three trips. Dumas hit safely twice in three at bats, both singles.

Blakely defeated Albany 2 to 1 at the Blakely home field, and Bainbridge at Dawson were postponed due to rain. The Albany loss and Arlington win created a tie at the top of the standings between these two teams. Dawson was in third followed by Blakely, Americus, and Bainbridge.

Tuesday, July 10, 1923

Circuit secretary and arbiter, N.P. Cornish of Savannah, Georgia, handed down a decision concerning the protested game between Blakely and Americus from July 5. Cornish ruled that Blakely manager Wallace Wade's protest was correct and that the game should be replayed as the first game of a double header at the meeting of the two teams next Saturday in Americus. This decision took one win away from Americus' record leaving it at four wins and eight losses and removed one loss from Blakely's making their record five and six.

Uncle Bob's bunch from Arlington blanked Americus on the Playground diamond 7 to 0 behind the strong pitching of Luther Bloodworth. Americus pitcher Lefty Owens allowed ten hits in the game including a home run by left fielder Smith in the third inning. Bloodworth struck out seven and walked two, while Owens fanned two, walked two, and hit one batsman. Offensively, Americus accumulated seven base hits, all of them singles. Third baseman Gid Wilkes got two of the hits for Americus in four trips to the plate, but he also booted two in the field.

Albany defeated Blakely on their home field by a 10 to 1 score. The very young Shaky Kain got the win over the twice his senior Goat Cochran. This turned out to be the only other game in the league for the day as Bainbridge at Dawson was rained out.

Wednesday, July 11, 1923

Arlington made it a clean sweep of the three game set with Americus winning the third game 6 to 5 in Arlington. Americus scored three runs in the top of the eighth to take the lead 5 to 3. The Bell Ringers answered all three runs in the bottom half of the inning and held on until the end. Red Laird took the loss for the Americus club giving up six runs on eleven hits, one walk, and no strikeouts, while Will Koenigsmark, who pitched eight innings, got no decision. Wally Norris pinch hit for Koenigsmark in the bottom of the eighth and pitched the top of the ninth winning the game. Pinkston got a two-bagger, Paul was two for four, and Dumas and Paul Collier both went three for four offensively for Americus.

Blakely upset the home team in Albany with an easy 10 to 3 victory. Miles pitched nine strong for Blakely while the Nut Crackers used Sam Boney, Greene Farrar, and Sheppard on the mound in attempts to cool the visitors' bats. Blakely manager Wallace Wade and second baseman Neil were both ejected from the game in the first inning for disputing a call "too vigorously."

Dawson took two games from Bainbridge at the Bainbridge diamond. Both games were one run games with the scores being 5 to 4 and 1 to 0.

Thursday, July 12, 1923

"Little danger exists that the Americus ball club will be disbanded before the season ends," manager Tom Bell was quoted in the Americus Times-Recorder. This statement came amidst rumors that the team was too financially strapped and the end of the organization was near. With a record of four wins and nine losses, the team was seeing a lower turnout at games than anticipated. A glimmer of hope came on the previous day when Americus played very well against a strong Arlington team. Fans were again optimistic about the Americus boys even though the game resulted in a loss. The directors of the team again canvassed local baseball enthusiasts for funds and raised enough, along with expected gate receipts, to stay afloat at least half of the remainder of the season. Bell reminded fans that if Americus is to remain a part of the fast South Georgia league, the cash must be fronted and the team must be supported. He was most certain that the local fans would not let the team fizzle.

After playing in only two games for Americus, catcher Howard Wright announced that he was leaving the team. Wright was supposed to be the savior of the struggling club, but his stay with the team was now being cut short. Getting one base hit in five at bats over two games, Wright's statistics were less than impressive in an Americus uniform. Barnhart would be moved back behind the plate from right field.

Americus was unsuccessful in preventing the team's fourth loss in a row as Blakely won 8 to 5 on the Blakely diamond. Goat Cochran got the win for the home team allowing eight hits, walking one, and striking out eight. Otis Bassinger took the loss surrendering eleven hits, no free passes, and issuing three strikeouts. The game was not a pretty one as Americus made six errors and Blakely made five. Four of the five runs for Americus were scored on errors while Fincher and Neil both homered for Blakely. Americus offensive highlights were a double for Eddie Wade, a triple each for Gid Wilkes and Dumas, and two stolen bases also for Dumas. Barnhart, Dumas, and Paul Collier each batted .500 in the game going two for four.

Albany paid Dawson back from the previous day by winning 10 to 2 on the Albany home field. Arlington won at Bainbridge 6 to 3, which allowed them to remain alone at the top of the league standings. Albany was only a half game behind in second place followed by Dawson, Blakely, Americus, and Bainbridge.

Friday, July 13, 1923

This Friday the thirteenth turned out to be a lucky one for the Americus team against the Blakely aggregation. On the Hardwood diamond, Americus batters pounded pitcher Hollingsworth for twelve hits as Americus won 9 to 5. Paul pitched the first six innings for Americus and was relieved by Red Laird. The two pitchers combined allowed only four hits on the day. Dumas, only needing a double to make the cycle, was the offensive hero for Americus going four for five with two singles, a triple, and a home run. Paul went two for five, and Collier was safe twice in four trips to the plate. Pinkston played an excellent game at second handling eleven balls without an error. The two teams were scheduled to play a double header Saturday.

Other games of the day in the South Georgia league saw Arlington win their seventh in a row at Bainbridge by a score of 6 to 2. Albany narrowly lost to Dawson, 7 to 6, at the Dawson field.

Saturday, July 14, 1923

In an exciting double header at the Playground diamond, Americus took two from the visiting Blakely team. Both games were blowouts with scores of 12 to 1 and 9 to 1. The first game was a makeup game of the protested, thrown-out game from July 5 between the two teams. Red Laird pitched masterfully for Americus allowing one run on three hits, one walk, and two strikeouts. Blakely pitcher/manager Wallace Wade was no secret to Americus batters who secured nine hits in the game that included a triple by Dumas and a double each by Paul and Bill Parsons. Dumas and Paul each also got a single both with four at bats in the game. First baseman Paul Collier also batted .500 in the game going two out of four. The game was fast and took only an hour and fifteen minutes to play.

The day's second game at the Playground saw Americus embarrass Blakely again. Miles started pitching for Hardwood but was relieved by Woodruff when Americus batters proved to be too much. Americus totaled eleven hits including five for extra bases. Dumas only had one hit in three trips, but it was a homer over the right field fence. Gid Wilkes had a triple and was two for four, Paul was two for three with a double, Paul Collier was a perfect two for two with a two-bagger, Big Bill Parsons got a double for his only hit in two trips. Barnhart and Collier each stole a base, and Lefty Owens got the easy win for Americus giving up three hits, one walk, and striking out three.

Arlington won their eighth game in a row at home against Bainbridge, 10 to 6. Albany lost to Dawson in Albany by a final of 4 to 3.

With three weeks under the belt of the South Georgia season, Arlington was at the top of the standings with a record of thirteen and five. Dawson's defeat of Albany broke the second place tie giving Dawson a half game lead over Albany. Dawson was eleven and six and one and a half games behind Arlington. Albany had eleven wins and seven losses, two games out of first. Americus held fourth place with seven victories and ten defeats putting them five and a half games out. Blakely held fifth place with a six and ten record, only a half game behind Americus. Bainbridge took the sixth slot with four wins and fourteen losses, three games behind Blakely and nine full games out of first place.

Sunday, July 15, 1923

"Shoeless" Joe Jackson was signed by Americus manager Tom Bell to play the remainder of the season with the team. Word of the signing of this famous "baseball outlaw" of the 1919 Chicago White Sox World Series scandal sent the entire South Georgia league into an uproar and threatened to break up the circuit. In a special meeting of the league directors held in Albany, vehement protest came from the other teams against Jackson playing for Americus. Representing Americus at the meeting was team director Rufus Lane who reported to Americus fans that the league felt that other players' careers would be jeopardized by playing with Jackson. Also present at the meeting were Dan Gibson of Albany, R.H. Bostwick of Arlington, W.S. Smith of Blakely, C.S. Haden of Bainbridge, and C. Dudley Cocke of Dawson. The directors voted five to one to bar Americus from playing Jackson. Baseball commissioner Judge Kenesaw M. Landis, who forever outlawed Jackson and seven other members of the 1919 Chicago White Sox from playing organized baseball again, was telegraphed by league secretary Dan Gibson to get his opinion on the matter of Jackson's eligibility.

Tom Bell found Jackson playing and managing under the name "Gus Johnson" for a team in Bastrop, Louisiana with, it was rumored, Eddie Cicotte, Buck Weaver, Swede Risberg, and possibly other expelled players from the 1919 Chicago team. Bell argued that since the South Georgia league was an independent organization and not under the jurisdiction of Commissioner Landis, Joe Jackson should be allowed to play as well as any other players who had been outlawed. The Americus fans stood tall behind Bell in the acquisition of Shoeless Joe. It was the general opinion of the fans that the other teams in the league were simply jealous that Americus was fortunate enough to secure the services of one of the greatest ball players ever, both with the bat and in the field. Ignoring the vote of the league, Bell announced that Jackson would be in uniform in Tuesday's game at the Playground when Dawson came to town. Bell went on to say that Americus would refuse to take the field if Jackson was not allowed to play.

25

Monday, July 16, 1923

Awaiting a reply from Judge Landis on the matter of Joe Jackson playing in the South Georgia league, Dan Gibson announced that Albany would withdraw their objection if Landis said Jackson was eligible to take the field. Albany's main objection to Jackson's playing was to protect the future playing careers of other players, especially pitcher Jack Slappey and first baseman Tot McCullough.

Rumors floated around Americus that Jackson was not the only baseball outlaw of the South Georgia circuit. It was said, but never confirmed, that the Albany club had two players and probably more who had been barred from organized baseball.

At a meeting held in a private dining room at the Windsor hotel in Americus, more than $1,500 was collected, including past pledges for subscriptions to the Americus baseball club, to support the team for the remainder of the season. Middleton McDonald presided over the meeting and Sam Coney acted as secretary. There were more than fifty fans present, and practically every one of them gave $25 or more. The fans at the meeting were enthusiastic that Americus should not only have a baseball team but should have a winning team.

Amidst the ruckus of Joe Jackson coming to the league, the games of the day took the back burner. The scheduled game of Americus at Dawson was postponed due to rain. Arlington kept their winning streak alive making it nine straight with a home win against Albany, 8 to 5. Bainbridge hosted Blakely and won by a narrow margin of 3 to 2.

Shoeless Joe Jackson celebrated his birthday turning thirty-four years old.

Tuesday, July 17, 1923

Shoeless Joe Jackson failed to arrive in Americus to play in the game against Dawson at the Playground diamond, but manager Tom Bell assured fans that he would reach Americus some time that night. As of game time on this day, the South Georgia league directors had not yet consented to Jackson playing for Americus. It was believed that the members of the league would come around and withdraw their oppositions to Jackson playing in time for Wednesday's game against Dawson.

Word reached Americus and the other cities of the South Georgia league from the office of Commissioner Landis that "any baseball player who willingly plays with or against any player expelled from organized baseball for conduct detrimental to baseball may find himself barred from organized baseball." J.H. Farrell, secretary of the

National Association of Minor Leagues, agreed with the Judge's boiler-plate statement saying that minor league clubs who belonged to that organization would probably not sign any players who had played with Jackson.

Another question was raised concerning Joe Jackson playing in an Americus uniform. Americus first baseman Paul Collier, formerly of Oglethorpe University in Atlanta, contacted Oglethorpe coach Frank Anderson inquiring about his future playing collegiate baseball if he played with Joe Jackson. Anderson replied that any college player who played with professionals in sports would be barred thereafter from playing in college athletics. The rule said that college players could play, during their summer vacation, against teams that had professional players, but they could not play on the same team as professionals. Collier had already decided that he would not return to college, but several other college players on the Americus team had to make a decision. There were quite a few college players on all the teams of the South Georgia circuit as well as a number of former professional players. Jackson's signing forced the league to take a hard look at the status of all players on all teams and clean the league out of college players who desired to return to play at school.

Yet another question surfaced after the college players playing with professionals rule was clarified. Was Joe Jackson still a "professional?" "Since he had been expelled from professional baseball, he was no longer considered to be a professional baseball player," many interpreted.

At the Playground diamond, Americus had hard luck against the Dawson aggregation with a final score of 5 to 3. Otis Bassinger, on the mound for Americus, surrendered eleven hits including a home run by Joe Burroughs, a triple by Ollie Marquardt, and four doubles by Kamisky, Rawson, Brunner, and Hines. Dawson pitcher Emmett Hines struck out ten Americus batters and gave up only five hits in the game. Bill Parsons, Bassinger, and Paul each got a double in the game to make up the offensive highlights for the home team. The win for Dawson put the team in first place in the South Georgia league standings.

The Arlington winning streak was finally broken at nine as Albany won on the Nut Cracker diamond 5 to 2. This game allowed Albany to make up a game in the standings on the now second place Arlington team. Blakely shutout Bainbridge in a slippery game at home, 3 to 0. The league now had Dawson at the top, Arlington in second, Albany third, and Blakely, Americus, and Bainbridge in fourth, fifth, and sixth places respectively. The race for first place was heating up as the end of the first half of the season came closer. Whichever team won the first half of the season would face the winner of the second half in the best of seven games league championship series to be played at the end of the season.

Wednesday, July 18, 1923

"Judge Landis is a good, honest man, and he will give a fair decision," Joe Jackson was quoted as saying upon his arrival in Americus. Jackson apparently had not yet been informed of the decision of Landis and Farrell. Shoeless Joe explained his move from the Bastrop, Louisiana team to Americus as "coming home again" as his residence at the time was Savannah, Georgia. In explaining the other teams' fear of him playing in the South Georgia circuit, Jackson summed it up by saying "What the boys are all unsettled about is not their future status as ball players, but that long bat I swing. They are simply making a tempest out of a teapot." Jackson's bat he was referring to was the famous "Black Betsy."

Jackson went on to explain his ineligibility and how his status would not affect the eligibility of other players he played with or against. "An ineligible ball player is ineligible, and that's all there is to it. Any player who has been expelled for jumping a contract or any other cause is just as ineligible as I am to play in the organized baseball ranks, and organized baseball has no jurisdiction over unorganized circuits. This was decided by Judge Landis, himself, long ago when objection was raised to my playing in Louisiana. No ruling has ever been made concerning the status of players belonging to organized ball teams who play with ineligibles in unorganized circuits." Jackson named a few players that he had recently played with in Louisiana who were now playing in the organized leagues. Red Hallman was now playing in the Cotton States League, and Eave Davis was now in the I.I.I. League. Neither of these players had had any bad experiences as a result of having been on a team with Jackson. In fact, both had received numerous complements on their excellent play that was a result of Jackson's tutelage.

Jackson also had several college players on his team in Bastrop including Lefty Wingard and Verdo Elmore both of the University of Alabama. The college players on the team recognize, it was said, that by accepting money to play baseball, even during their summer vacation, they were in violation of the collegiate athletics rules and were no longer eligible to play at the college level.

In a telegram received at the Americus Times-Recorder from the Sporting News in St. Louis, Missouri, word was conveyed that Americus was running the risk of never again being allowed to enter future teams into the realm of organized baseball if Joe Jackson plays. The telegram read "Both Landis and Farrell intimate that independent players associating with Jackson and his kind will never later be allowed in organized baseball, and also to blacklist any city that employs crooked players, including Americus."

Julius Shy of Americus received information via telegram that Joe Jackson isn't the only ineligible player signed up in the South Georgia league. Arlington star pitcher Luther Bloodworth had been declared ineligible after failing to show up to pitch for the Columbia, South Carolina club of the South Atlantic Association after signing a contract to play the 1923 season. It was argued that the league could not allow Bloodworth to continue to pitch and prevent Joe Jackson from playing as both players are classed the same in eligibility.

Americus lost to the Dawson team, 8 to 6, on the wet Baldwin Park diamond in a seven-inning hitting display by members of both teams. Americus was leading 6 to 4 going into the bottom of the sixth inning when Dawson rallied and scored four runs. Red Laird pitched strong through five innings but began to weaken in the sixth. After pitching into a jam, Laird was replaced on the hill by Lefty Owens who did not fare any better. The winning pitcher was Cassares, who was pitching in his first game for the Dawson team. Americus accumulated nine hits, two of which were home runs by center fielder Eddie Wade in his two at bats. Gid Wilkes and Paul each got a double going one for four and two out of three respectively, and Dumas stole a base. Pinkston got a pair of base hits in four trips to the plate. Dawson hitters struck for eleven hits including a homer and a double off the bat of center fielder Rosenfeld.

Albany defeated Arlington, 7 to 2, to make the race for first place in the first half more interesting. Arlington ace Luther Bloodworth, whose eligibility was now in question, took the loss for Arlington on his own diamond, and Greene Farrer earned the win for the visitors. The league stood with Dawson in first by a one game margin over Arlington and Albany who were tied for second. Blakely was in fourth at five and a half games behind first, Americus in fifth at six and a half out, and Bainbridge in sixth at seven and a half games out of first. It was becoming a very tight race for first between the top three teams with only four more games for each left in the first half of the season.

BASE BALL

BAINBRIDGE

IN

AMERICUS

Friday and Saturday

July 20th and 21st

Joe Jackson Has Arrived

Reached Americus Wednesday morning and will be in Americus uniform Friday afternoon. You may come expecting to see the famous Joe. Also other players who were with Jackson in Louisiana are enroute here but it is not known whether or not they will reach Americus in time for Friday's game.

Remember the second half of the season starts Monday and Americus is determined to win this second half AND the pennant. Our team has been materially strengthened and with a little BOOSTING instead of knocking from the fans you will be doing you part to help win.

GAME CALLED AT 4 P. M.

Ad that appeared in the July 19, 1923 edition of the Americus Times-Recorder

Thursday, July 19, 1923

Robert C. Lane, a director of the Americus club and former Mercer University player, sent a telegram J.H. Farrell, secretary of the National Association of Minor Leagues asking if there had ever been a ruling with reference to ineligible players playing with prospective players that would affect their eligibility in the future. Farrell replied that "every individual player's standing must be investigated and passed upon separately. Free agents are not affected after investigation."

Since every player in the South Georgia circuit was considered a free agent without current ties to any organized baseball clubs, then playing with Joe Jackson would not affect their future status. Neither Landis' nor Farrell's office had any jurisdiction over the players of the South Georgia circuit or the circuit itself. The six teams in the league took a vote for the final word on whether Jackson would play or not. The vote was 3 to 2 in favor of Jackson playing. Americus, Arlington, and Blakely voted in favor, Bainbridge and Dawson voted against, and Albany abstained. At last, the objections to Shoeless Joe suiting up for Americus were withdrawn. It was announced that Joe Jackson would definitely be in an Americus uniform in Friday's game against Bainbridge at the Playground diamond.

Americus traveled to Bainbridge and was greeted with a loss, 6 to 2. Paul was on the mound for Americus surrendering nine hits, three free passes, striking out two, and taking the loss. Red Moseley's pitching for the home team was the feature of the game giving up only four singles to Americus batters. First baseman Pickett and outfielder Sheppard both made several excellent plays in the field.

Dawson shutout Arlington at home, 2 to 0, while Albany at Blakely was a rainout. Dawson stayed atop the league, and their defeat of the Bell Ringers allowed the idle Albany to slide into second place. The rest of the league rankings went Arlington, Blakely, Americus, and Bainbridge in order.

Friday, July 20, 1923

Shoeless Joe Jackson's name was finally in the lineup for the Americus baseball team after several long days of ifs and buts. Approximately six hundred fans turned out at the Playground diamond in Americus to see the famous ex-big-leaguer play. Jackson's uniform was described as white flannel with the American flag embroidered on each of the long sleeves. Just being in the lineup seemed to give the other Americus players and the fans added morale.

Americus was facing Bainbridge in the game, and manager Tom Bell put Jackson in left field and lined him up to bat fourth. Shoeless Joe gave the fans their money's worth when he gunned down Bainbridge shortstop Arnold at home trying to score from second on a grounder hit to left in the fifth inning. It was Jackson and his famous "Black Betsy" bat that provided the most excitement when he hit the first pitch he saw from Bainbridge hurler Swann deep to center field for a triple. Jackson's other hit in the game was a double, and he ended up going two for five on the day.

In Americus Line-Up Today

Picture of Joe Jackson from the July 20, 1923 edition of the Americus Times-Recorder

The final score of the game was Americus 9, Bainbridge 4. Lefty Owens started the game for Americus but began to get wild and was relieved by Red Laird in the fourth. Swann was the starting pitcher for Bainbridge but was replaced by Red Moseley in the third after Americus scored five runs. Besides Jackson's two extra base hits, Bill Parsons got two doubles in three at bats, shortstop "Smith" went three for five, including one two-bagger, and scored twice, and catcher Barnhart was two for five.

Several mysterious names appeared in the lineup on Shoeless Joe's first day on the field for Americus. Most are believed to be the regular players who wanted to take the field with Jackson but did not want to jeopardize their futures. The names "Dillon," "Jones," and "Smith," were in the lineup, but they are believed to have actually been regular players using fake names. Dillon is believed to be third baseman Gid Wilkes, Jones was the assumed name used by center fielder Eddie Wade, and Smith was actually shortstop Dumas.

Other action in the South Georgia league included a double header between Blakely and Albany in which Albany took both games at the Hardwood diamond. The first game was a pitcher's dual with a final of 1 to 0 while the second game ended in a 9 to 2 score. Arlington narrowly defeated Dawson 2 to 1 at the Dawson home field. The two wins for Albany were crucial for the team to stay alive in the race for first. Arlington helped their own cause by defeating Dawson, but Albany got a boost from it too. The standings now, with one game to go in the first half of the season, were Dawson in first with a fourteen and seven record. Albany in second with fifteen wins and eight losses, the Bell Ringers of Arlington in third, one full game out of first at fourteen and nine, Blakely's seven and thirteen record held fourth, Americus was tied with Blakely with the same record, and Bainbridge in last place with seven wins and fifteen losses.

At a meeting of the directors of the Americus baseball team, the entire club was reorganized. In order to permit the most thorough reorganization, at the beginning of the meeting, all members of the board of directors submitted their resignations. This group included Nathan Murray, Robert C. Lane, Theron Jennings, Thomas L. Bell, W.W. Ray, A.C. Crockett, Rufus Lane, Lovelace Eve, and H.P. Everett. A new managing committee was now named that was made up of Nathan Murray as Chairman, Rufus Lane as a director, and Thomas L. Bell as another director. A.C. Crockett was elected secretary-treasurer, Stuart Prather as assistant treasurer, Robert C. Lane in charge of ticket sales, Sam Coney and Alton Codgell as transportation committee, Theron Jennings and W.W. Ray as advertising committee, and Ernest Pantone and Charles Smith as the grounds committee. The new directorate decided that Joe Jackson would be made the team's field captain in charge of players and Tom Bell would remain the team's manager.

Arlington catcher, Jimmie Clements, who played in the first game of the regular season for Americus, came forth to clarify the situation concerning the ineligibility of pitcher Luther Bloodworth. Clements had been closely associated with Bloodworth for the past five years and felt compelled to set the record straight to keep his friend's name clean. Immediately after graduating from Mercer University, Bloodworth signed to play for Columbia, South Carolina of the South Atlantic Association but never reported to play. Columbia placed Bloodworth on the voluntary retired list while he played amateur baseball that summer. The following spring, Bloodworth went to

Columbia and played two games for the club. It was this action, "playing against ineligibles while on voluntary retired list" that caused J.H. Farrell's office to declare Bloodworth ineligible. Farrell also ruled that Bloodworth would be eligible to play in organized baseball again if he paid a fine of $200. The argument of Luther Bloodworth being eligible or ineligible had already been put to bed when the league members agreed that organized baseball had no jurisdiction over the circuit.

JOE JACKSON
Positively Will Play Here
TODAY AND SATURDAY
Rufus Lane wired Club at noon today from Albany- "Joe Jackson will play with Americus--- Advertise this at once."---Rufus Lane

BASE BALL

BAINBRIDGE
IN
AMERICUS
Friday and Saturday
July 20th and 21st
GAME CALLED AT 4 P. M.

Ad that appeared in the July 20, 1923 edition of the Americus Times-Recorder

Saturday, July 21, 1923

The race for first place for the first half of the South Georgia circuit season came down to the wire, and the Nut Crackers of Albany came out on top. Arlington had to beat Dawson for the second time in three games, and Albany had to be victorious over Blakely for the third game in a row in order for Albany to win the first half pennant. Arlington did defeat Dawson at the Arlington field by a score of 2 to 0. Blakely succumbed to Albany 6 to 2 in an exciting contest at Albany. The Bainbridge at Americus game, which was won by Americus, 6 to 5, had no effect on the three-team race for first between Albany, Arlington, and Dawson. The first half standings ended with Albany in first with sixteen wins and eight losses and filling the slot as one of the two teams to play for the league championship at the end of the second half. Dawson was one game back at fourteen and eight. Arlington took third only one percentage point behind Dawson with a record of fifteen and nine. Americus was a distant fourth by a six and a half game margin between them and first with eight wins and thirteen losses. Blakely came out in fifth at seven and fourteen and seven and a half games behind first. Bainbridge took last place in the league with a seven and sixteen record and eight and a half games behind Albany.

In Joe Jackson's second day in an Americus uniform, he went two for two and was walked twice on purpose in the ten-inning game against Bainbridge at the Playground diamond. Americus came out on top 6 to 5 after a fast and exciting game. "Giddens" and Jackson scored in the Americus half of the first on three straight doubles by Giddens, Jackson, and Wade. Bainbridge answered in the top of the second with two and one more in the third. With the score now 3 to 2 in the bottom of the third, Americus tied it up on two doubles by Giddens and Randolph. The game went back and forth until Americus tied it at five in the bottom of the eighth as catcher Walton scored on two singles and a fielder's choice. No more runs came until the bottom of the tenth when Americus third baseman Giddens connected for a double scoring pitcher Otis Bassinger from first to win the game. Bassinger got the win giving up five runs on ten hits, three walks, and three strikeouts. Yank Roberts got the loss for Bainbridge on giving up twelve total hits. Offensively for Americus, Jackson was two for two with a double, Giddens was three for five with a double, Randolph was also good three out of five times, and Walton got two base hits in three trips to the plate.

Two more "mystery names" appeared in the Americus lineup. "Giddens," who played third base and had an outstanding day with the bat, was actually Isben "Gid" Wilkes who played under the name

Dillon on Friday. Gid, the nickname Wilkes went by everyday, was short for Giddens, his middle name. "Randolph" also was in the Americus lineup playing shortstop only for this game. He is believed to actually be Pinkston, the regular shortstop.

The second half of the season was set to begin on July 23 and run for four weeks. It promised to be fast and furious since the acquisition of Shoeless Joe Jackson by Americus as other teams were scrambling to find additional talent.

Sunday, July 22, 1923

With the first half of the season being a disappointment to the Americus fans, the club decided to seek out new talent for the second half. The signing of Shoeless Joe Jackson was a definite boost for the team, but the directors wanted to recruit more high-quality ball players to insure that the team would be the best in the South Georgia league. Instead of looking high and low for a player here and a player there, Jackson told the directors that he knew of practically a whole team of first class ball tossers who were up for hire. The team he was speaking of was his previous team in Bastrop, Louisiana. The Bastrop players of the independent, traveling team were so good that they were unable to keep games scheduled because of the embarrassment they caused their opponents. All the teams Bastrop was playing in Louisiana were canceling games and disbanding making it difficult to keep the club afloat. Each man was a top-notch player, Jackson described, and they were all in need of employment for the rest of the summer. The Americus club directorate thought the idea to be excellent and told Shoeless Joe to get these players to Americus. After talking to the Bastrop players, Jackson, now the Americus team captain in charge of players, made the announcement of the roster shake up. New players, who arrived in Americus Saturday night, included second baseman Bill Nolan, third baseman Bill Williams, left fielder Verdo Elmore, first baseman Otis "George" Brannan, shortstop Johnny Lindsey, catcher Polly Duren, and pitchers Ernest "Lefty" Wingard, Red Hallman, Davenport, and H.F. Benson. The only players who were retained from the first half of the season roster were center fielder Eddie Wade, right fielder Bill Parsons, catcher Barnhart, and pitcher Red Laird. Jackson announced that the starting lineup for Monday's game would most likely be Nolan, 2B; Williams, 3B; Elmore, LF; Jackson, RF; Brannan, 1B; Wade, CF; Lindsey, SS; Duren, C; and Wingard P. It was noted in the Americus Times-Recorder that several of the players brought their wives with them to Americus and that their coming was expected to add interest to a number of social affairs around town.

36

BASEBALL

Americus
Vs.
Albany

Tuesday, July 24
4 p. m.
At Play Ground Diamond

(This space donated by Times-Recorder.

Ad that appeared in the July 23, 1923 edition of the Americus Times-Recorder

Monday, July 23, 1923

The second half of the South Georgia league season started well for Americus as the team defeated Albany 5 to 4. It was called "Too Much Jackson" at the Albany diamond as Shoeless Joe led the offense going two for three with a two-run homer. With all new players in the lineup for Americus with the exception of Eddie Wade in center field, Americus won the eventful game in the ninth inning. Down by one run, Verdo Elmore got to second when the Albany shortstop kicked one into left field. Joe Jackson followed beating out a bunt that sent Elmore to third. George Brannan was up next and singled to right scoring Elmore to tie and sending Jackson to third. Eddie Wade came to the plate next and drove in Jackson for the winning run on a ground out to second. Ernest "Lefty" Wingard got the win for Americus in his first appearance giving up eight hits, walking two, and striking out three, while Albany's young Shaky Kain took the loss on seven hits, two walks, and four strikeouts. Offensively, Bill Williams and Elmore got a double each for Americus both going one for four, and Jackson was two for three both being singles. Defensively, the infield turned a textbook five-six-three double play during the game. The new and improved Americus team was called the fastest outfit seen by the Albany fans, and predictions were that Americus would easily win the second half pennant.

In other league action on the first day of the second half, Dawson traveled to Bainbridge and handed the home team a shut out, 3 to 0. Blakely played host to Arlington only to be defeated by the Bell Ringers 5 to 3.

Tuesday, July 24, 1923

Seventeen hundred fans filled the bleachers of the Playground diamond to see Americus defeat Albany for the second time in as many days by a final of 11 to 2. The bats were hot for Bill Williams and Verdo Elmore, both three for four on the day, and Bill Nolan hit safely in two of his four at bats. But the big hitter of the game was shortstop Johnny Lindsey who batted 1.000 in four trips to the plate including a two-run home run in the eighth inning. Red Hallman got the easy win for Americus defeating Albany's Greene Farrer who received little run support from his team. Although Joe Jackson was the big drawing card for Americus, he was by no means the entire show. The Americus club certainly now had its share of quality ball players that were going to create much difficulty for opposing teams.

In other South Georgia circuit games, Blakely, with several new faces in the lineup, defeated the Uncle Bob's club at Arlington, 3 to 1. New players for Blakely included pitcher Lucas "Terrible" Turk, second baseman George Thrasher, shortstop Gid Wilkes, second baseman Pinkston, both formerly with Americus, and outfielder Roy Jenkins, formerly of Macon of the South Atlantic League. In the third game of the day, Bainbridge narrowly won from Dawson, 5 to 4, at the Bainbridge diamond.

R.C. Moran published an article in the Americus Times-Recorder in response to a previous article written in the Atlanta Journal Constitution newspaper by Morgan Blake. Blake called Joe Jackson an "ignorant, illiterate fellow" in a slamming article that attempted to cast a dark shadow across Jackson and the Americus baseball team for employing him. Blake attacked the integrity and honesty of Joe Jackson, the directors and management of the Americus club, and the Americus fans who backed the team. In his article in the Times-Recorder, R.C. Moran stood up for these men and Jackson by saying "these Americus gentlemen know something about the men who constitute the team, and the fans here have faith in their integrity -- whatever any writer may think or say to the contrary."

Wednesday, July 25, 1923

After winning four games in a row since Shoeless Joe took the field for Americus, the team finally lost a game. Albany hosted Americus and won 6 to 5 as Jack Slappey gave up nine hits, struck out ten, walked one, and held Joe Jackson to one single in four at bats. Davenport got the loss for Americus pitching in relief of Red Laird. Albany scored two runs on Davenport in the bottom of the eighth that gave them enough to win. Barnhart and Bill Williams were both two for four on the day, Bill Nolan got a two-base hit, and Verdo Elmore was credited with a stolen base. George Brannan and Johnny Lindsey turned a three-six-three double play in the game showing off the impressive Americus defense, but the Albany bats were just too much to hold off. Americus' record was now two and one for the young second half of the season.

Bainbridge was downed by Dawson, 9 to 6, in the third game of their three-game set in Dawson. Arlington at Blakely was rained out.

Thursday, July 26, 1923

Approximately one thousand fans turned out to the Arlington diamond in Joe Jackson's first appearance there. The final was 7 to 2 with Americus being the victor behind the masterful pitching of Lefty Wingard. Wally Norris, on the mound for the Bell Ringers, also pitched well, but the five errors by him and his team allowed Americus to win the game. George Brannan, Johnny Lindsey, and Polly Duren all were two for three in the game, and Brannan also stole a base. Joe Jackson was held to only one double in three trips to the plate, but he thrilled the Arlington fans with one of the longest balls ever hit at the local diamond. It was fortuitous for the home team that the ball went foul.

Albany defeated Bainbridge in other league action 8 to 2 in a sloppy game played at the Nut Crackers' home field. Bainbridge's right fielder Parrish had the big hit of the game when he belted one over the right field fence. Blakely and Dawson played to a nail-biting seven all tie. Dawson, the home team, tied the game in the bottom of the eighth by scoring six runs. The game was marred when the Blakely team started many squabbles for stalling in hopes of holding off until it got too dark to play. Dawson was threatening with a man on second and two outs when the umpire called "ball game."

The rumor mill was hard at work in the South Georgia league especially in the league's largest city of Albany. Many fans were repeating rumors that some of the players on the Americus team were actually Buck Weaver, Eddie Cicotte, Swede Risberg, and other outlawed, former major leaguers. A special meeting of the league's directorate was called at which all players on the Americus roster were revealed and closely examined. It was agreed that Joe Jackson was the only player on the team who was an "outlaw" and also the only player who had ever played in the major leagues. Some of the team's players had only played as high as the college level while others had played minor league and/or semi-pro baseball. Albany vowed not to quit just because Americus had a winning team with a star player in the form of Shoeless Joe Jackson. They further vowed to "strengthen up" their squad for the rest of the season and give the strong Americus team something to fear on the diamond.

Friday, July 27, 1923

Americus manager Tom Bell announced that arrangements were being made for the Americus team to play a number of outside games at the end of the South Georgia league season. The decision was made to play a post-season, traveling schedule so that other Georgia cities outside the South Georgia circuit could have the pleasure of seeing Joe Jackson play. More bids were coming in to Bell's office every day, and many were offering as high as five hundred dollars a day to see Shoeless Joe play. Jackson consented to play for the team in the post-season outside the circuit so that as many as possible could be gratified by seeing him play baseball.

Five errors by the Americus infield were blamed for losing the game to the Arlington Bell Ringers at Uncle Bob's diamond. Luther

Bloodworth fooled many Americus batters allowing only four hits in the 5 to 1 victory. Red Hallman took the loss for Americus and was relieved by Paul in the sixth inning of the seven-inning affair. Joe Jackson got two of the Americus hits in his three at bats, and Bill Williams scored the only run.

Bainbridge hosted Albany and won in a fast game, 2 to 1. Bainbridge pitcher Yank Roberts got the win over Albany's Shaky Kain. Bainbridge catcher Angley broke his finger in the first part of the game and was replaced by Charlie Gibson. Angley was not expected to return to the lineup. The scheduled game of Arlington at Blakely was postponed by rain.

Saturday, July 28, 1923

All nine men in the Americus lineup hit safely at least once during the game at the Playground ball field as Bainbridge lost to Americus 9 to 2. Bainbridge scored both of their runs in the first inning but could not get any more throughout the rest of the game. Davenport was on the mound for Americus allowing six base hits, striking out five, and walking none. The losing pitcher for Bainbridge was veteran Red Moseley who was relieved by Hamilton in the sixth inning. Bill Williams and Polly Duren each got a double for the home team, and Johnny Lindsey was credited with a stolen base going two for four on the day. Joe Jackson had the high batting average for Americus with two singles in three at bats.

Blakely was victorious at home as Dawson came to town. The final score was a narrow 2 to 1 in the pitcher's dual. Arlington traveled to Albany for the day's third game of the South Georgia circuit where the two teams tied at four runs each.

At the end of the first week of the second half of the season, Americus, with a record of four wins and two losses, was tied with Dawson, record of two and one, for first place. Arlington and Dawson were a half game behind the league leaders both having two wins and two losses. Albany was one game out of first with a two and three record, and Bainbridge was in last at two and four.

Monday, July 30, 1923

An announcement was made of a benefit game to be played on the upcoming Thursday at the Playground diamond. The "cause" of the game was to raise extra funds to cover expenses incurred beyond budget on a recent road trip by the Americus team. "A number of pretty girls are cooperating with the club directors in the sale of these tickets," the article in the Times-Recorder read. The fans were being asked to pay $1 for this special game when Albany was coming to town. Over two thousand fans were expected to turn out to the game.

Rumors were floating all over the South Georgia league about the high salaries of the players on the Americus team. Claims were coming from all over that every player on the Americus team was being paid $75 a week or more. Robert C. Lane, a director of the Americus club, denied reports that any player on the team received more than $75 per week. Shoeless Joe Jackson was the highest paid player on the team, Lane reported, and his salary was, in fact, $75 a week. Salaries were ranging between $40 and $75 a week with an average that was around $60 per week. "The salary list and payroll of the team is open to inspection of any interested person, and an inspection of the club records will dispel any doubts anyone may have regarding the salaries paid for players here," Lane was quoted as saying. Lane also mentioned that the league did not have any salary limits that teams could pay players and that Dawson and some of the other teams were paying players as high as $100 per week to play.

In a laugher of a game, Americus defeated Dawson 15 to 2 at the Playground. Lefty Wingard had the right stuff on the mound for Americus giving up eight scattered hits, walking two, and striking out six. First baseman George Brannan was the only Americus player to not get a base hit in the game, but Bill Nolan and Verdo Elmore picked him up getting three hits each in six and five at bats respectively. Bill Parsons was three for five with two doubles, and Bill Williams went two out of five, also with two two-baggers. Joe Jackson was two for five with a double and scored three times. The big inning for Americus was the third when eight runs were scored while the team batted a round plus four. Pitcher Emmett Hines took the loss for the visiting Dawson team.

Arlington hosted Bainbridge in a pitching contest at Arlington. The final was 3 to 1 as Arlington's Tige Stone allowed four hits as he out pitched Hamilton and Hecker of Bainbridge combining to allow only two hits. All of Arlington's three runs were unearned and results of errors. Albany and Blakely played another low-scoring pitcher's dual of a game in Albany where the final was 2 to 1 in favor of the home team. Jack Slappey got the win for Albany while Buddy Williamson took the hard loss for Blakely.

Baseball In Americus

Tomorrow

WEDNESDAY—August 1 st 4 P. M.
Americus vs. Dawson

--ALSO--

THURSDAY—August 2, at 4 P. M.
Americus vs. Albany.
FRIDAY—August 3 at 4 P. M. Americus vs. Albany.

Come and see the greatest baseball machine outside the big leagues – See a game for 50 cents that's worth $2. See the mighty Joe Jackson knock 'em over the fence and peg home plate from deep center

3 Games More at Americus This Week 3

Ad that appeared in the August 1, 1923 edition of the Americus Times-Recorder

Tuesday, July 31, 1923

Shoeless Joe made his first appearance on the Dawson diamond as Americus easily defeated the home team 8 to 2. Dawson scored one run in the first inning, but Americus got two in the fifth and five more in the sixth. Joe Jackson only needed a double to hit for the cycle going three for five in the game. Bill Parsons hit safely twice in four at bats, and Polly Duren was two for five. Red Hallman allowed four hits, one walk, and struck out five earning his second win in three games pitched since coming to Americus. Dawson pitcher Sullivan took the loss allowing Americus nine hits in the game.

Bainbridge blanked Arlington 7 to 0 at the Bainbridge field. Blakely hosted Albany and lost by a 9 to 3 final.

Wednesday, August 1, 1923

The powerful Americus team won their fourth game in a row as they finished a three-game sweep of Dawson. The final was 10-7 at the Playground ball yard as Joe Jackson was hitless on the day due to four intentional walks in his five trips to the plate. The big stick for Americus was first baseman George Brannan who sent one over the fence with the bases loaded in the first inning. Dawson left fielder Shorty Poore also hit a two-run homer with Ollie Marquardt on base in the eighth inning of the highly offensive contest. Shortstop Johnny Lindsey batted 1.000 in three at bats with two doubles. Third baseman Bill Williams also got a double in a two for two day, and right fielder Bill Parsons was also perfect at the bat with three singles in three trips to the plate. Dawson pitcher Pfeiffer allowed twelve hits, struck out four, and issued eleven walks as he got the loss in the game. Davenport got the win for Americus and was relieved after seven innings by Red Hallman. Verdo Elmore, who pinch-hit for Davenport in the eighth made the fourth Americus batter to bat 1.000 in the game going one for one.

Bainbridge made the trip to Arlington and won by a 5 to 3 final score on a wet diamond. The crowd was small due to the bad weather as Hamilton pitched his way to a win for Bainbridge. Baby Wilder, on the mound for Arlington, pitched very well but was defeated because of four errors by the Arlington defense. Blakely shelled Albany 10 to 3 at the Albany field as pitcher Greene Farrer allowed the visitors eighteen hits including home runs by Hardwood left fielder Roy Jenkins, right fielder Polly Pounds, and pitcher Dick Lowery.

A week and a half into the second half, Americus held a commanding lead over the rest of the league. With a record of seven and two, Americus was two and a half games in front of second place Albany who had four wins and four losses.

Thursday, August 2, 1923

Americus began a scheduled three game set against Albany by extending their current winning streak to five games. The final score was 5 to 4 at the Playground ballpark in Americus before a large crowd who paid extra to see this special benefit game to help pay for Americus' travel expenses. Lefty Wingard was on the mound for Americus while Albany surprised the home team by pitching "Big Bill" Statham, a famed Southern League pitcher, under the assumed name of "Hicks." Americus struck first with three runs in the bottom of the second inning that included a home run by pitcher Wingard. Americus scored one more run in the fifth making the score 4 to 0. Albany had a big inning in the sixth scoring four runs on three base hits and three Americus errors. Johnny "Bunny" Lindsey, Americus shortstop, was credited two of these errors that tied the game at four runs each. In the bottom of the ninth with the score still tied and one man out, Wingard hit a double and was pushed over to third on a single by Bill Nolan. Shoeless Joe was coaching third and stopped Wingard from going home on Nolan's hit not wanting to take a chance. Third baseman Bill Williams came up next and singled to left driving in Wingard to win the game. Offensively for Americus, Wingard was two for four with a homer and a double, Joe Jackson was two for three with a triple, Verdo Elmore was two for four with a double, Nolan was two for five with a double, Eddie Wade got a double, and Lindsey stole a base. Wingard also won his fourth game in as many starts for the Americus team giving up eight hits, walking two, and striking out four. Bill Statham/Hicks took the loss for Albany on eight hits, one walk, and two strikeouts.

In the game of Dawson at Bainbridge, the home team was victorious 3 to 2 in an exciting, well-played ball game. Blakely hosted Arlington for two games, both of which were won by Blakely. The first game was high scoring with a final of 9 to 6. A pitcher's dual is what the second game turned out to be as the final was only 1 to 0. These two wins moved Blakely solidly into second place behind Americus in the South Georgia circuit standings.

Baseball In Americus

Tomorrow

Friday--August 3 at 4 p.m.

Americus vs. Albany

Come and see the greatest baseball machine outside the big leagues—See a game for 50 cents that's worth $2. See the mighty Joe Jackson knock 'em over the fence and peg home plate from deep center.

1 Games More at Americus This Week 1

Ad that appeared in the August 2, 1923 edition of the Americus Times-Recorder

Friday, August 3, 1923

The Americus winning streak was ended at five games as Albany won at the Playground 3 to 2. Red Hallman, on the mound for Americus, and Shaky Kain, pitching for the Nut Crackers, both pitched very well throughout the eleven-inning contest. The hits and runs were scattered for both teams, but Albany scored the winning run in their half of the eleventh and held on to win the game. Polly Duren and Bill Williams both got doubles for Americus, and Verdo Elmore went two for four. Approximately one thousand, eight hundred fans were in attendance. Hallman, taking the loss, allowed three runs on eleven hits, three walks, and five strikeouts. Kain won the game for Albany and surrendered two runs on seven hits, walking two walks, and fanning two.

Arlington blanked Blakely, 5 to 0, at the Arlington ball yard as pitcher Wally Norris pitched masterful ball allowing only three hits from the visitors. Norris' cause was helped by the excellent defense of the Bell Ringer infield and a home run by third baseman Consuello Smith. Pitcher "Terrible" Turk got the loss for Blakely and was relieved in the sixth by Hap Henderson.

Bainbridge garnered eleven hits off of Dawson's pitcher Pfeiffer on their home field winning the contest 8 to 2. Yank Roberts got the win for Bainbridge behind excellent run support including a five-run fifth inning. Umpire Evans stopped the game in the fifth for one minute as a tribute of respect for President Warren G. Harding who had passed away on August 2.

Saturday, August 4, 1923

An altercation between Albany pitcher Jack Slappey and catcher Bill Kimbrell was blamed for the loss to Americus at the Albany baseball field. Americus won 4 to 2 in the contest that was marred by a nasty exchange of words between the Albany battery in the sixth inning. Slappey was unable to regain his composure afterwards and walked in a run with the bases loaded. Two innings later, Americus had tied the game up at two, and Slappey again walked in a run with the bases loaded giving Americus a 3 to 2 lead. Americus third baseman Bill Williams hit a solo homer in the top of the ninth for some insurance for the visitors. Williams was also three for five on the day with a double, and Joe Jackson was two for three rounding out the offense for Americus. Pitcher Davenport got the win allowing eight Albany batsmen to reach base safely, walked one, and struck out one. Jack Slappey got the loss allowing four runs on seven hits, six walks, and eight strikeouts. The Americus defense turned three exciting double plays in the game that went Brannan to Lindsey to Nolan, Elmore to Williams, and Davenport to Nolan to Burroughs. During the game, Reverend James Turner of the First Baptist Church in Albany led a moment of silence in remembrance of the late President Harding.

In other South Georgia circuit games, Uncle Bob's gang of Arlington defeated Blakely by the slim margin of 2 to 1 at the Hardwood baseball park. Bainbridge handed the Dawson baseball aggregation their seventh consecutive loss in a 3 to 2 contest.

At the half way point of the second half of the season, Americus, nine wins and three losses, held a two-game lead over second place Bainbridge, who was seven and five. Third place was occupied by Blakely with an even record of five and five, three games behind first place. Albany had gone from fifth place at the end of the first week of the second half, up to second place by mid-week, and then back to fourth by the week's end with a five and six record, three and a half games out of first. Arlington was tied with Albany with the same win-loss record, and Dawson struggled in last place with two wins and eight losses and six full games behind first.

Monday, August 6, 1923

With the close of the South Georgia season less than two weeks away, the announcement came that teams could not add any new players after August 13 to their rosters, or if new players were added, they would not be allowed to play in any post-season games. This rule was made to prevent team from bringing in outside talent to try to strengthen their team just for the championship series. Albany was already assured the first slot in the best of seven league championship series as they had the best record of the first half of the eight-week season. Americus was favored to win the second half behind the guidance of Shoeless Joe Jackson.

Arlington rang the Americus bell for fifteen runs and nineteen hits in a blowout contest on the Arlington diamond. The final score was 15 to 6 as Americus used three pitchers. Lefty Wingard started the game for Americus but was pulled in the fifth for Davenport to finish the inning. Red Laird pitched the rest of the game in which Wingard suffered his first loss in an Americus uniform. Tige Stone was on the mound for Arlington and held Americus to only seven hits. Stone also hit a two-run homer in the fifth inning. For Americus, Bill Williams was three for four with a triple and a double, Joe Jackson was three out of five with two doubles, and Johnny Lindsey got the only other

Americus hit with a single. Bob Lightfoot and Ike Thrasher both went four for five on the Arlington side.

Albany shutout Dawson, 4 to 0, at the Dawson home field. "Hicks", real name Bill Statham, got the win for Albany while Grunt Lucas took the loss for the home team. Bainbridge hammered Blakely 11 to 5 in Blakely to round out the day in the South Georgia league.

Tuesday, August 7, 1923

Americus pitcher Red Hallman pitched perfect baseball through six innings as Americus defeated Arlington 4 to 3. Arlington, playing on their home field, was unable to get a man on base until the seventh inning when two runs were scored on a walk and three consecutive singles. Hallman allowed only four hits, walked two, and struck out eight batters in the game. Luther Bloodworth was on the mound for Arlington allowing ten hits, walking five, and striking out six in a game that featured excellent pitching from both sides. Another interesting fact about the game was that both teams played errorless baseball throughout the entire game. Shortstop Johnny Lindsey was credited one stolen base, left fielder Verdo Elmore got a double, Joe Jackson went three for four, George Brannan was two for three, and Bill Parsons got two hits in four trips to the plate. A second game was played in which Arlington beat Americus 3 to 2, but it was for exhibition only and did not count in the league standings.

Blakely was victorious over Bainbridge, 6 to 4, in a slow game on the Bainbridge home field. Buddy Williamson got the win for Blakely, and Konneman took the loss for Bainbridge. Albany pitcher Shaky Kain was shaken up by the Dawson team for eight runs in the third inning as Dawson upset Albany 12 to 7. Dawson had finally ended their eight-game losing streak in the game played on the Albany diamond. Pfeiffer was the winning pitcher, and Kain, who was relieved by Mitchell after three, got the loss for Albany.

Wednesday, August 8, 1923

In a one-sided game played on the Playground field in Americus, Arlington was slaughtered by the home team 13 to 0. Shoeless Joe Jackson made the defensive play of the game with a backward running catch in deep center field that robbed Arlington center fielder Bob Folmar of a home run. The catch was called by many present the most spectacular catch ever made on a minor league diamond. Jackson and his bat, "Black Betsy," also starred at the plate with a grand slam home run in the third inning. Wally Norris started the game pitching for the visitors but was pulled after five innings for Baby Wilder. Davenport got the easy win for Americus allowing seven hits, walking one, and striking out seven improving his record to three and one. A crowd of approximately sixteen hundred fans watched as every Americus player in the lineup got at least one base hit. Bill Nolan went three for four with a double, Verdo Elmore was four for five with a double, Jackson was two for four with a homer, Johnny Lindsey was three for five with one two-base hit, and Polly Duren was two out of three on the day.

The struggling Dawson team was defeated by Albany, 7 to 5, at Baldwin Park in Dawson. Shaky Kain, on the mound for Albany, was in great form for five innings, but had to be replaced in the sixth when he lost control. Hicks/Statham was brought in to complete the job, but Kain had already secured the win. Sullivan was the losing pitcher for Dawson.

Bainbridge won at Blakely in a slow contest by a final of 5 to 2. Interestingly, all five of Bainbridge's runs were scored in the fifth inning, and both of Blakely's runs were scored in the seventh. Terrible Turk got the win, and Yank Roberts took the loss.

At the end of the games played in the South Georgia circuit, reports were floating around that the Arlington and Dawson teams had decided to disband. This could not be confirmed at the time, and no official word had yet come from the league directors. Arlington was in fifth place with a six and eight record at the time, and Dawson held last place, seven games behind first place Americus, with three wins and ten losses.

Thursday, August 9, 1923

In the day's only game played in the South Georgia league, Americus and Bainbridge played to a 4 to 4 tie. Americus evened the score in the bottom of the ninth at the Playground diamond by scoring three runs. The last-chance rally that prevented the Americus loss was started by Shoeless Joe hitting a solo homer with one out. George Brannan batted next and got a double followed by Joe Burroughs, who was picked up from Dawson, pinch-hitting for Bill Parsons, who also got a two bases. Brannan was held at third and did not score on Burroughs' two-sacker. Eddie Wade struck out next, but Polly Duren picked him up with a two-out double to deep left field that drove in Brannan and Burroughs to tie the game. Lefty Wingard ended the inning with a ground out to short. Umpire Evans called the game for darkness after Americus' final batter of the inning leaving it tied in a knot. Wingard pitched beautifully for Americus allowing only four hits, walking three, and striking out eleven. Konneman started the game for Bainbridge but was relieved by Hamilton in the eighth. Brannan went two for four with a double, Duren was also two for four with both hits for two bases, and Bill Williams and Burroughs got one double each.

Blakely at Dawson was rained out as was Arlington at Albany.

Friday, August 10, 1923

Uncle Bob Bostwick's Bell Ringers of Arlington ceased to exist officially as the club disbanded. The team was financially strapped and had been stagnant in fifth place for the last two weeks. It was expected that Dawson would fold next for many of the same reasons. Dawson had been in last place in the South Georgia circuit for the last two weeks, and the attendance had naturally fallen off. Also, Dawson's next scheduled series of games was against the now defunct Arlington. The team was not expected to be able to survive financially being if they were idle and without revenue for four consecutive days.

Americus traveled to Bainbridge for the second game of a three-game set and played to a tie for the second consecutive day. The final was a perfect 5 to 5 with each team also garnering nine hits and making one error. Motts started the game pitching for Americus and was relieved by the newly acquired Luther Bloodworth in the seventh inning. Bloodworth failed to save the game for Motts when he allowed Bainbridge to score two runs in the bottom half of the ninth. Watts was the starting pitcher for Bainbridge, but he was relieved by Hamilton to finish the game. Bill Williams had the hot bat for Americus with three hits in four at bats including a double. Johnny Lindsey was two for five, and Bill Parsons went two for four. Shoeless Joe Jackson was held hitless, but he was intentionally walked twice in the game.

The "orphaned" Arlington club was shutout 8 to 0 at the Albany diamond. Orion Mitchell got an inside-the-park home run when the left fielder over ran a liner. Jack Slappey got the win for Albany while Tige Stone was the losing pitcher. Stone was commended for piecing together nine players to make a showing at the Albany game. Even Uncle Bob Bostwick suited up and manned first base for the noble nine of Arlington. So busy was Stone to get enough men to make a team that he didn't warm up properly. This was evident when Albany got four runs in the first frame.

Although most likely on the way out to pasture, Dawson showed life in a home-field double header against Blakely. Dawson won both of the pitcher's dual games, 2 to 0 and 2 to 1. Grunt Lucas was on the mound for Dawson in the first game and allowed only two hits. Bill

Ellis took the loss on the hill for the Hardwood allowing seven hits and walking nine. In game two, Pfeiffer was victorious for Dawson allowing four hits and striking out six. Goat Cochran got the loss for Blakely allowing only three hits but giving up two runs. The two wins were morally boosting for Dawson, but not enough to pull the struggling team out of the cellar.

Saturday, August 11, 1923

The announcement came that the Dawson baseball club of the South Georgia league was officially disbanded. The league was now down to four teams: Albany, Americus, Bainbridge, and Blakely. With only seven game days left in the season, the remaining four teams would only have to slightly modify their schedules to finish the season without interruption.

In a masterful display of pitching by Americus pitcher Red Hallman, Americus shutout Bainbridge 5 to 0 in the Bainbridge ball park. Hallman allowed only three hits, struck out eleven, and issued only one free pass in his fourth victory in an Americus uniform. Americus bunched three runs in the third inning and two in the fifth with eight of their nine safeties also coming in these innings. The batting honors of the game went to Americus local "Big Bill" Parsons who hit two doubles in three at bats. Bill Nolan was two for four with a double in the game, and Joe Burroughs was also two out of four with a double. Johnny Lindsey, Nolan, and George Brannan combined for a six-four-three double play in the game.

Blakely was scheduled to host Dawson, but the game was cancelled due to the Dawson defunct. Arlington was scheduled to play at Albany, but Tige Stone could not get another piece-meal nine together forcing cancellation of the game.

With one week left in the season, Americus held a comfortable lead in first place with twelve wins and four losses. Bainbridge was in second place by three games with a record of nine and seven. Albany was only a half game behind Bainbridge with an eight and seven record. Blakely took fourth place, which was now last place in the league, with a six wins and nine losses and five and a half games out of first.

Sunday, August 12, 1923

An exhibition game was played between Americus and Blakely in Montgomery, Alabama to let baseball enthusiasts in that neck of the woods see Shoeless Joe Jackson perform. Americus won the game that did not count in the South Georgia circuit standings, 3 to 1. Lefty Wingard, an Alabama native and former player of the University of Alabama, was on the mound for Americus and allowed six hits, struck out three, and walked one. The pitchers dual would have probably been a tie with one run each if not for the three errors committed by the Hardwood shortstop Wagoner. Pitcher Dick Lowery, who took the loss, also made a fielding error that could have been blamed for one of the Americus runs. Shoeless Joe made one of his famous back-handed catches on a hit by Blakely catcher Meyers that would have been a triple with any ordinary center fielder on the job. None of the Americus batters got more than one hit, and Wingard got the only extra-base hit with a double. A small crowd of Americus fans made the trip to Montgomery stopping along the way to pick up fans from Blakely, Dawson, Cuthbert, and Union Springs.

Monday, August 13, 1923

The final week of the South Georgia league season began as former Arlington moundsman Wally Norris, who was picked up after the demise of the Bell Ringers, pitched excellent baseball for Americus. About one thousand fans turned out to the Playground diamond to see Americus defeat Blakely 3 to 2 in the shortened, six-inning game. The contest was abbreviated because the two teams played a Sunday game for exhibition in Montgomery, Alabama the day before instead of having the day off. Norris allowed only four hits, walked one, and struck out five in his first start for Americus. His counterpart on the Blakely side, Goat Cochran, gave up seven hits, walked two and struck out eleven batters accounting for over sixty percent of the putouts by the Dawson defense. First baseman George Brannan was two for two on the day, Norris was two for three with a double, and Bill Williams and Joe Jackson got a double each in the contest.

The other game of the South Georgia league saw Albany defeat Bainbridge in Albany by low-scoring 2 to 1 final. Bainbridge's lone tally was a home run from the bat of third baseman Wheeler in the ninth inning. Long, on the mound for Bainbridge got the loss, while Hicks/Bill Statham got the win for the Nut Crackers.

The Macon Peaches of the South Atlantic League picked up pitcher "Grunt" Lucas, who formerly pitched for Dawson. Lucas hurled a two-hit shutout on August 10 against Blakely.

BASE - BALL

AMERICUS
VS.
BLAKELY

Tuesday, Aug. 14

3:30 P. M.

At Play Ground

Ad that appeared in the August 13, 1923 edition of the Americus Times-Recorder

With a record of thirteen wins and four losses, Americus needed only one more win before the end of the season to make it to the league championship against first half winner Albany.   Third place Bainbridge, nine and eight, would need to win every game from here on out, and Americus would have to lose the rest of their games if Bainbridge had a shot at post-season play.   One more win would not secure the pennant for the second half for Americus, only the second slot for the league championship. The rules were that the first half winner would play the second half winner at the end of the season for the title of South Georgia league champion. In the case that the same team won both halves, the runner up of the second half would get to play the pennant winner for the post-season crown.

Tuesday, August 14, 1923

Americus easily defeated Blakely for the second day in a row extending the Americus winning streak to four games and securing the second slot in the South Georgia circuit championship series. With a final score of 4 to 1 at the Playground, the game was marred by bad calls from Umpire Erskine Mayer. Americus third baseman Bill Williams was ejected from the game when he vehemently insisted that Mayer had called a play incorrectly. Mayer did, however, make it fair by making equally rank calls against both teams. Luther Bloodworth was pitching for Americus and got the win giving up six hits, walking none, and fanning seven. Buddy Williamson took the loss for Blakely giving up seven hits, three walks, and striking out three. Joe Jackson had the big hit of the game in the form of a two-run homer in the seventh inning. Jackson also struck out for the first time since coming to Americus when he watched the payoff pitch go by. Many present believed the wide pitch to be ball four, and Umpire Mayer heard these judgments from the stands as well as many other comments about his officiating capabilities. Joe was very well known for connecting with most any pitch that was anywhere close to being "over," as he would describe pitches. If he wasn't swinging, it wasn't over, fans commented. Left fielder Verdo Elmore was the only Americus batsman to garner more than one hit going two for four. George Brannan got a triple, and Bob Folmar and Johnny Lindsey each got a double. An exciting and unusual one-two-six double play was turned by Americus, Bloodworth to Polly Duren to Lindsey.

Bainbridge traveled to Albany and was defeated 11 to 8. Bainbridge's third baseman Wheeler and Albany's initial sacker Tot McCullough each hit home runs in the game.

Americus now held first place over Albany by three and a half games. With fourteen wins and four losses in the second half, Americus would have to lose rest of their games, and Albany, with ten wins and seven losses, would have to win the remainder of their schedule in order for Americus to not win the second half pennant. Regardless, with the victory over Blakely on this date, Americus secured the second slot in the South Georgia league championship series against first half winner Albany.

Wednesday, August 15, 1923

A coin was tossed to determine where the first game of the South Georgia league championship series, also being called "The Little World's Series," would be played between Albany and Americus. Joe Jackson made the call correctly for Americus and chose to have the home field for the first game. Games would then alternate between the two cities until one team had won four out of seven games. Following the coin toss, Americus manager Tom Bell and Albany manager/player Milton Reed exchanged rosters to make official the players who would be eligible to play in the series. Albany's roster had Reed, Kimbrell, Eldridge, Cooper, Mitchell, McCullough, Holland, Farmer, Slappey, Hicks/Statham, Cain, Cameron, and Cochran. The Americus roster consisted of Jackson, Brannan, Nolan, Lindsey, Williams, Duren, Elmore, Wingard, Hallman, Bloodworth, Norris, Davenport, Williamson, Burroughs, Folmar, Parsons, and Barnhart. The umpires for the post-season games had not yet been named. The directors of the Americus and Albany teams could not agree on two umpires that met the satisfaction of both clubs.

Additional bleachers were being added to the Playground ballpark to seat between seven and eight hundred more fans for the upcoming league championship series. It was announced that no automobiles would be allowed on the field because of lack of space. Admission to games in Americus and Albany were fixed at 75 cents for adults, 35 cents for children, and 50 cents for blacks.

Americus traveled to Blakely and lost in a sweltering slugfest, 9 to 8. The run getting started early with Americus getting four on the board in the top of the first. Blakely answered with one in the second and five in the third. The Hardwood gang led most of the game with the score being tied once in the seventh inning at seven. Down nine to seven, Americus scored one run in the top of the ninth, but Blakely quickly snuffed out the rally. Americus pitched Davenport, Lefty Wingard, Wally Norris, and even Joe Jackson in efforts to try to stop the Blakely bats that garnered fifteen hits in the game. Blakely started with Bill Ellis on the mound and later Dick Lowery who, combined, allowed twelve Americus hits. Ellis got credit for the win, and Norris took the loss being the pitcher of record when Blakely took the lead. Bill Williams took the batting honors for Americus going three for five, Verdo Elmore was two for five with a triple, Bob Folmar was also two out of five, and Jackson went one for two with a double and two intentional walks.

Albany beat Bainbridge in the other South Georgia game, 5 to 3, at the Bainbridge home field. Albany center fielder Orion Mitchell and

Bainbridge right fielder Parrish each hit balls that cleared the fence. Jack Slappey got the win for Albany while Yank Roberts took the loss for the home team.

Thursday, August 16, 1923

Americus won the pennant for the second half of the South Georgia league season by taking the first game of a double header against Bainbridge 8 to 1. The second game at the Bainbridge diamond was won by Americus as well, 7 to 1. Bainbridge celebrated their last home games of the season with barbecue for the fans, and attendance was estimated at over three thousand. In the first game, Americus second baseman Bill Nolan had a career day with the bat going five for five, all of them singles. Shortstop Johnny Lindsey was three for five with a stolen base, and pitcher Red Hallman hit safely twice in five at bats. Joe Jackson got a double and Bob Folmar got a triple. Hallman was the game's winning pitcher allowing eight scattered hits, walking one, and fanning eight. Hamilton got the loss for Bainbridge and was relieved by Konneman half way through the game. In the second game of the twin bill, Lefty Wingard was the winning pitcher allowing only five hits, no free passes, and striking out six. Long was the losing pitcher for the home team surrendering eight hits, walking three, and issuing six strikeouts. Verdo Elmore carried home the batting honors going two for three with a double and a triple. Jackson was also two out of three in the game, and Nolan was credited one stolen base.

The South Georgia circuit's other game of the day was Blakely at Albany. Blakely won 8 to 5, but the highlight of the game was a fifth-inning fight between Blakely pitcher Dick Lowery and Umpire Young Evans. The altercation started when Lowery claimed that an Albany base runner had interfered with Blakely shortstop Gid Wilkes' fielding of a hit. When Evans refused the claim, a violent exchange of words began, and Lowery was ejected from the game. Lowery would not leave the field and continued to argue when Evans lost his temper completely and hit Lowery with his mask. Other Blakely players had joined in the scuffle, and police officers were called to the field to restore order. Albany police chief Wallis made court cases against both men and ordered them both to leave the ball park. Evans claimed that Lowery provoked the fight by calling him a "vile name" several times.

BASE - BALL

AMERICUS
VS.
BAINBRIDGE
Friday, August 17
3:45 P. M.
At Play Ground

*Ad that appeared in the August 16, 1923 edition of the Americus Times-Recorder
The advertised game was cancelled when Bainbridge failed to show.*

Reverend James B. Turner, pastor of the Albany First Baptist Church, was called upon to take the umpire's indicator and serve as arbiter for the remainder of the game. Lowery got no decision, George Clarke got the win in relief, and Hicks/Statham took the loss. Albany center fielder Jack Farmer and Blakely right fielder Winn hit a home run each in the contest. Farmer was part of Albany's "bulking up" for the post-season having played for Pittsburgh of the National League in 1916 and for Cleveland of the American League in 1918. Albany had also acquired infielder Harry Holland, a former star of the Atlanta Crackers.

Friday, August 17, 1923

The scheduled game of Bainbridge at Americus was cancelled when word reached Americus at game time that the Bainbridge club had disbanded the night before. Games were scheduled between the two teams for Friday and Saturday to finish the second half of the season, but it looked now like Americus could start preparing for "The Little World's Series" that was scheduled to start Monday, August 20. To not totally disappoint the fans that turned out, a pick-up game took place that consisted of picked teams among nine Americus players and nine local people from the stands. This game was played under the agreement that no score would be kept.

Albany easily shutout Blakely at the Albany diamond by a final of 7 to 0. Jack Slappey got the win, and Goat Cochran took the loss.

Saturday, August 18, 1923

The regular season of the South Georgia baseball league wrapped up with Albany defeating Blakely 10 to 3 at the Albany ball yard. Americus was idle as their scheduled game with Bainbridge was cancelled the day before.

Americus cakewalked through the second half of the season taking the pennant with a sixteen and five record. Albany was runner up in the second half with thirteen wins and eight losses and three games behind Americus. Bainbridge took third place seven games behind first with a record of nine and twelve. The noble team from Blakely, who finished out the season, took fourth place by eight games with eight wins and thirteen losses. Arlington and Dawson could be considered to have placed fifth and sixth respectively based on their records before they both disbanded.

"The Little World's Series" was set to start in Americus Monday, August 20. Additional stands were being built in Albany and Americus to handle the crowds of three to five thousand fans that were expected at each game. Earlier in the season, the caliber of baseball played in the South Georgia league was compared to that of the class D leagues, the lowest echelon of organized baseball. Now, the experts

59

were saying the league's brand of ball was comparable to the class B baseball being played in the South Atlantic League.

Monday, August 20, 1923

　　With the first game of the league championship series scheduled to begin at 3:45 p.m., Americus manager Tom Bell spent the morning lobbying for a last-minute change of umpires. At the meeting held the previous Wednesday, the officials for the series couldn't be agreed on as Albany wanted Umpires Erskine Mayer and Young Evans who had served the league since the start. Bell's opposition was mainly toward Evans who had gained the reputation among Americus fans as being incompetent. Fearing bad calls and low fan turnout at the games played in Americus, Bell said he would accept any umpires other than these two. Tom Bell met with Evans before the start of the first game of the series and asked him to decline to officiate. Evans refused to agree to this at which time Bell brought up the incident of last Thursday in which Evans struck Blakely's Dick Lowery with his mask. It was rumored that a pistol dropped out of the pocket of Evans during the scuffle, but it had been resolved that the gun came from the pocket of a deputy sheriff who was breaking up the fight. Bell also asked Evans about reports of his drinking while on the job, but Evans denied these reports. Not being satisfied but realizing that the officials were not going to change by their own accord or any one else's, Tom Bell resigned his position and any affiliation with the Americus baseball club. To insure that the officiating maintained integrity, a committee was named to monitor the umpires during the series with the authority to remove an umpire from service at any time and to reverse any decision when the rules of baseball were in clear violation. Manager Bell named J.W. Hightower of Americus to this committee, and Albany manager Milton Reed named H.F. Haley to serve.

　　With more that two thousand fans on hand at the Playground diamond, the game was played with each umpire making only one objectionable call each. Witnesses said that both calls were favorable to the Albany team, but the supposed bad judgments did not help the visitors as Americus won the game 5 to 1.

　　Leading off in the top of the first inning for the visiting Nut Crackers was manager/third baseman Milton Reed who flew out to Joe Jackson in right. The next Albany batter was shortstop Harry Holland hitting a double off pitcher Red Hallman to right field. Center fielder Jack Farmer came up next and grounded out to third. Tot McCullough, first baseman, hit a single back to the pitcher moving Holland over to third. Right fielder Orion Mitchell made the third out of the inning grounding to short and stranding two runners.

Americus came to bat in the bottom of the first with usual lead off man second baseman Bill Nolan who grounded out to short. Third baseman Bill Williams, the second batter up for the home team, struck out. Left fielder Verdo Elmore drew a two-out walk from pitcher Hicks/Bill Statham as the third batter, and Joe Jackson, playing right field, was also walked. With men on first and second, first baseman George Brannan hit a long ball over the right field fence to put three Americus runs on the board. With a score of 3 to 0, center fielder Bob Folmar ended the inning by striking out.

In the top of the second inning, Albany's catcher Bill Kimbrell flew out to short. Left fielder George Clarke, whose playing was protested against because his name was not on the certified list of players turned in the prior week, grounded out to second. Second baseman Ollie Marquardt hit one for two bases to Elmore in left field, but he was stranded by Hicks/Statham on an infield fly to short.

Shortstop Johnny "Bunny" Lindsey led off the bottom of the second with a pop fly to right field for the first out. Catcher Polly Duren got on base lining one to left. Pitcher Red Hallman flew out to right. Nolan got a free pass to first after being hit by a pitch moving Duren over to second with two outs. Williams made the third out on a drag bunt fielded by the catcher.

Reed struck out for the first out in the top of the third frame. Holland drew a walk. Farmer went down swinging for out number two, but Holland stole second during this at bat. McCullough hit a liner to center for a single, and Holland scored from second making the score 3 to 1. Mitchell was walked next moving McCullough to second. Kimbrell grounded to Lindsey at short throwing to Nolan covering second forcing Mitchell out to end the inning.

With a two run lead, the home team came to bat in the bottom of the third. Elmore led off with fly out to center field. Jackson hit safely to left for one base. Brannan popped up to center for the second out. Folmar moved Jackson over to third with a single to center, but Lindsey ended the inning with a grounder to short.

The Albany half of the fourth went one-two-three with Clarke striking out, Marquardt flying out to the pitcher, and Hicks/Statham grounding out short to first.

Just as quickly went the Americus half of the fourth. Duren struck out, Hallman grounded out to second, and Nolan flew out to left field.

Milton Reed led off the middle inning for Albany with a pop up to second baseman Nolan for the first out. Holland was fanned by

61

Hallman's slants. Farmer legged out a single hit to short but became the third out on a fielder's choice at second off the bat of McCullough.

Williams got to first safely on a liner to right to begin the bottom of the fifth. Elmore got a single to short next. Jackson grounded out to short for the first out. Brannan made out number two going down on strikes, and Folmar flew out to center stranding two on base.

Three pop flies from the Albany bats completed the top of the sixth. Mitchell, Kimbrell, and Clarke flew out to Elmore, Jackson, and Elmore again respectively.

Americus put one more tally on the board making it 4 to 1 in the bottom of the sixth inning. Lindsey led off with an unsuccessful bunt fielded by the catcher. Duren was next getting a double to left. Hallman flew out, and Duren went to third on the tag. Nolan came through with a triple to deep center field scoring Duren. Williams batted next and made the third out on a grounder to Marquardt at second.

Nut Cracker batters were set down in order for the second inning in a row in the top of the seventh. Marquardt and Hicks both were fanned, and Reed popped out to Williams in foul territory.

In the bottom of the seventh, Americus sent seven batters to the plate and scored once to make it 5 to 1. Elmore led things off with a single to left. Jackson made it safely to first on a fielder's choice putting Elmore out at second. Brannan made the second out on a pop up to right field. Folmar drew a walk moving Jackson over to second. Lindsey had a clutch single next that scored Jackson and moved Folmar to second. With the score now 5 to 1, Duren singled to shallow left, not deep enough to score Folmar. Hallman ended the inning for Americus on a grounder to first with Hicks covering.

The top of the eighth was yet another three up, three down inning for the cold Albany bats. Holland flew out to Jackson in right, Farmer grounded out to Brannan at first unassisted, and McCullough copied Holland with a pop fly to right.

Americus batters went down in order in the bottom of the eighth for only the second time in the game. Nolan flew out to right, Williams fanned, and Elmore grounded out short to first.

The visiting Albany team was unable to push any runs across in their last chance to save the game. Mitchell made it safely to first when shortstop Lindsey booted what should have been an easy out. Kimbrell flew out to Jackson in right, Clarke struck out, and Marquardt flew out to right to end the game.

Red Hallman, who won five games for Americus in the second half of the season, got the victory in game one allowing only five hits, two walks, and striking out seven. Hicks/Statham took the loss for the visitors allowing eleven hits, walking three, and striking out five. Polly Duren went three for four, all singles, and Verdo Elmore was two for four, both singles. George Brannan had the biggest hit of the game with a three-run home run in the bottom of the first. The second game of the South Georgia league championship series was scheduled for Tuesday in Albany.

Tuesday, August 21, 1923

An article appeared in the Albany Herald newspaper explaining why the Albany baseball club held out for Young Evans and Erskine Mayer to be umpires in the Little World's Series. Albany's club directorate supported these two to officiate the post-season games because they had been calling games for the South Georgia league since it started. It was only fair to allow those who had faithfully served the league throughout the regular season to be rewarded by umpiring the post-season games. Americus manager Tom Bell had originally wanted to have John Wagnon of Americus and one official who Albany would name instead of Evans and Mayer. The article continued to say that players on both teams supported Evans and Mayer and that Bell was the only one who was opposed to them. Further went the write-up saying that Albany, too, had had disagreements with Evans, especially when he ejected Milton Reed early in the first game of a double header previously in the season. Feelings concerning the altercation with Dick Lowery were mixed as some sympathized with Evans saying he was provoked and other saying he should have exercised forbearance. Many Americus fans did not agree with this article, and much uproar and criticism of Evans came from the stands in game two of the series.

Over two thousand fans, about one-fourth from Americus, crowded the Nut Cracker's ball park to see game two of the Little World's Series. The Americus fans really got their money's worth as Americus handed Albany their hat with a 19 to 4 routing.

Second baseman Bill Nolan led off the top of the first for the visiting Americus team with a fly out to right field. Third baseman Bill Williams jumped on an easy pitch from Jack Slappey and sent it over the fence making the score 1 to 0. Left fielder Verdo Elmore got a single to left next. Right fielder Joe Jackson ended the inning by grounding into a four-six-three double play.

In the bottom of the first, Albany's manager/third baseman Milton Reed led off with a pop out to right field. Shortstop Harry Holland made it safely to first on an error by third baseman Williams.

Center fielder Jack Farmer struck out, and initial sacker Tot McCullough grounded out to pitcher Lefty Wingard.

Americus took the second inning by storm scoring five runs and batting all nine players. First baseman George Brannan led things off with a single to right. Center fielder Bob Folmar was next reaching safely on an error by Marquardt. Shortstop Johnny Lindsey got a single to third but Brannan was unable to score. Catcher Polly Duren batted next sacrificing to left scoring Brannan from third to make the score 2 to 0. Pitcher Lefty Wingard came up next hitting what was called one of the longest balls ever hit at the Albany diamond for a three-run home run. The score was now 5 to 0. With the bases now empty again, Nolan flew out to right for out number two. Williams was up next and hit his second home run in as many at bats improving the Americus lead to 6 to 0. Elmore got a single on a liner to left field, and Jackson ended the inning by flying out to Eldridge in left.

The Nut Crackers had no luck at all in the bottom of the second as the batters went down in order. Right fielder Orion Mitchell flew out to Jackson, and catcher Bill Kimbrell and left fielder Harry Eldridge both went down on strikes.

Three more runs were pushed across by Americus in the top of the third inning. Brannan led it off with a pop out to left. Folmar followed legging out a single to short. Lindsey hit a single to left field moving Folmar over to third. Duren fouled one back to the catcher for the second out. Wingard got a single to left pushing Folmar across making it 7 to 0 and moving Lindsey to third. Nolan got to first safely on an error that allowed Lindsey and Wingard to score. With the score now 9 to 0, Williams ended the inning on a grounder third to first.

The bottom of the third saw Albany go in order again. Second baseman Ollie Marquardt grounded out to second, pitcher Jack Slappey flew out to center, and Reed grounded out to pitcher Wingard.

With clouds looming overhead, Americus threw away the top of the fourth trying to get the game officially in so it would count as a series win. Elmore flew out to center, Jackson was out on an easy grounder to first, and Brannan, on what was a base hit, went out at third after purposely not stopping at first or second. Albany changed pitchers during the inning bringing in Bill Ellis to relieve Slappey. The change was also used to stall for time in hopes that the rain would come before enough innings could be played to make the game count.

In the bottom of the fourth, Albany finally got on the scoreboard. Holland led off the inning with a walk. Farmer followed being hit by a pitch. McCullough was next and was safe at first on a fielder's choice that put Holland out at third. Mitchell made it to first safely on a liner to center scoring Farmer from second making the score

9 to 1. Kimbrell was up next with a hit to left driving in McCullough and making it 9 to 2 and sending Mitchell to third. With one out, Eldridge sacrificed Mitchell across the plate to make the score 9 to 3. Marquardt ended the inning on a fielder's choice that put Kimbrell out at second.

Americus threw away another inning in the top of the fifth with clouds threatening to dampen the easy win. Folmar grounded out to short, and Lindsey and Duren both struck out.

Albany was unable to get any hits off of Lefty Wingard in the bottom of the fifth. New pitcher Bill Ellis flew out to left. Reed grounded out to first unassisted. Holland drew a walk but was stranded when Farmer grounded out the third.

With the threat of rain diminishing, the top of the sixth was again productive for the visiting Americus team. Wingard led off with a single to left. Nolan followed with a fly out to right field. Williams was safe at first on a fielder's choice that put Wingard out at second. Elmore got a single to center that moved Williams over to third. Jackson and his "Black Betsy" bat followed with a three-run homer over the left field fence increasing the Americus lead to 12 to 3. Brannan made the third out on a grounder to second.

Three men went to the plate and back to the bench for Albany in their half of the sixth. McCullough softly grounded out to Nolan at second. Mitchell popped up to Nolan, and Kimbrell ended it with a grounder to first.

Another big inning was had by Americus in the top half of the seventh. Folmar started the batting beating out a ground ball to third. Lindsey was next with a free pass. Duren made the first out on a lazy fly to center field. Wingard got a single on a liner to left that scored Folmar making it 13 to 3. Nolan was out number two on a grounder second to first that pushed Wingard and Lindsey to second and third. Williams got a base hit to left that drove in both base runners making the score 15 to 3. Elmore followed with a three-base hit that pushed Williams across the plate from first. With the score now 16 to 3, Shoeless Joe hit his second homer of the game over the right field wall driving in Elmore and making the score now 18 to 3. Brannan made the third out for Americus on a slow roller to first unassisted.

Left fielder Eldridge led off the Albany half of the seventh with a base hit to left. Marquardt was next flying out to center field. Ellis made it to first safely on a fielder's choice that forced Eldridge out at second. Reed made the third out on a lazy fly ball to Elmore in left.

The top of the eighth inning only saw four Americus batters come to the plate. Folmar led off the inning with a ground out to second. Lindsey followed with the second out popping up to short.

Duren lined a single to right field, but he was stranded there when Wingard made out number three on a ground ball Marquardt to McCullough.

Albany batters went down in order in the bottom of the eighth with Wingard doing most of the defensive work. Holland led off with a strike out, and Farmer and McCullough both grounded to the pitcher who threw on to first.

Americus went into the top of the last frame leading off the top of the order. Nolan made it safely to first when center fielder Farmer dropped a fly ball. Williams was next with fly out to right. Elmore followed with a single to left that moved Nolan over to third. Parsons batted in the fourth slot for Jackson and was thrown out at second trying to stretch a single into a double. Parsons drove Nolan in making the score 19 to 3. Brannan ended the visitor's turn with a ground out to second.

In Albany's last chance to salvage the game, right fielder Mitchell led off with a long solo home run over the center field fence. Pitcher Wingard recomposed himself and set the rest of the batters down in order. Kimbrell grounded out to second, and Eldridge and Marquardt both popped up to second baseman Nolan ending game two of the series 19 to 4.

Lefty Wingard got the win for Americus allowing only four hits, striking out five, and walking two. Jack Slappey took the loss for Albany being relieved by Bill Ellis in the fourth. Right fielder Orion Mitchell had the big hit for Albany with his ninth-inning, solo homer. Every Americus player in the game with the exception of Bill Parsons garnered at least one base hit. Verdo Elmore had the highest average on the day going five for six with a triple. Wingard had the second highest percentage with four hits in five at bats including one round trip. Joe Jackson and Bill Williams were both three out of six and each hit two home runs in the game. George Brannan and Johnny Lindsey each got two hits, and Polly Duren had one double.

Americus now held a two games to none lead in the Little World's Series over Albany. Game three was scheduled to be played Wednesday afternoon at the Playground in Americus.

BASEBALL

"The Little World's Series"

Albany at Americus

WEDNESDAY

Games called promptly at 3:45 p. m.

AT AMERICUS PLAYGROUND
ADDITIONAL SEATS PROVIDED

Ad that appeared in the August 21, 1923 edition of the Americus Times-Recorder

Wednesday, August 22, 1923

Game three of the South Georgia league championship series was a reversal of the routing that Americus handed Albany in game two. Albany, not letting the 19 to 4 loss from game two get them down, easily defeated Americus at the Playground diamond by a final of 12 to 4. Approximately fifteen hundred fans paid to see the game, very few from Albany after the embarrassment of the previous day. The Nut Crackers fans that did attend got their money's worth as their club disabled Americus from sweeping the series making it now two games to one.

Albany got two runs in the top of the first inning partly because of two errors by Americus shortstop Johnny Lindsey. Manager/third baseman Milton Reed led off reaching first safely on the first of Lindsey's boots. Reed advanced to second on a wild pitch by Buddy Williamson. Shortstop Harry Holland was the second batter and walked. Lindsey made his second error on Jack Farmer's at bat when he threw wild to second trying to get Holland in the force. Farmer was safe at first, Holland safe at second, and Reed scored making it 1 to 0. First baseman Tot McCullough bunted one back to Williamson who couldn't field it cleanly filling the bases. Right fielder Orion Mitchell

67

made out number one on a sacrifice grounder to short that scored Holland to make it 2 to 0. Catcher Bill Kimbrell was safe at first on a bunt to the pitcher that put Farmer out at the plate. Harry Eldridge, playing left field, walked next filling the bases, but second baseman Ollie Marquardt stranded all three runners by ending the inning on a pop up to second.

The first three batters of the game went in order for the home team. Second baseman Bill Nolan led off grounding to first with the pitcher covering. Third baseman Bill Williams struck out and was thrown out at first when the catcher dropped strike three. Out three came when left fielder Verdo Elmore grounded out short to first.

After batting one man short of a round in the first, Albany led off the top of the second with pitcher Floyd Kroh drawing a walk. Reed, up next, also got a free pass as did Holland to load the bases. Farmer came through next with a ground rule double that got stuck in the right field canvas driving in Kroh and Reed making it 4 to 0. McCullough made the inning's first out on a grounder to second. Mitchell got a hit on a liner to center field scoring Holland and sending Farmer to third. Now a 5 to 0 game, Kimbrell was safe first on a bad hop error by second baseman Lindsey who let the ball go between his legs. Eldridge made out number two on a sacrifice fly to center that scored Farmer on the tag. With the score 6 to 0, the inning ended on a fielder's choice off the bat of Marquardt in which Mitchell was out at third.

Joe Jackson, playing right field, led off the bottom of the second with a double to left field. First baseman George Brannan grounded out to second, and Jackson advanced to third. Center fielder Bob Folmar went out pitcher to first, and Jackson dashed home shocking the defense that he would run on the play. The score now 6 to 1, shortstop Johnny Lindsey ended the inning fanning to Kroh.

Kroh led off again in the top of the third after Albany batted all nine in the second. All three batters flew out in this inning with Kroh going to left, Reed to second, and Holland to short.

Americus also went three up, three down in the bottom half of the third. Catcher Polly Duren led off with a pop fly to center field, pitcher Buddy Williamson grounded to third, and Nolan flew out to Marquardt at second.

Farmer was first up for Albany's half of the fourth and got a single to right. McCullough was safe on a fielder's choice forcing Farmer out at second. Lindsey, trying to turn a double play, made his fourth error of the day when he over threw first allowing McCullough to reach second. Mitchell was up next getting a double to left and scoring McCullough to make it 7 to 1. Kimbrell made out number two on a ground ball to first unassisted, and Mitchell advanced to third. Eldridge drove Mitchell in on a legged out single to short. Eldridge ended up at second on another one of Lindsey's overthrows. Albany's half of the inning ended at 8 to 1 when Marquardt flew out to Nolan at second.

The bottom of the fourth started with a hot single through the box from the bat of Williams. Elmore was up next with another single. Jackson popped up to third for the first out holding the runners at first and second. Brannan also flew out on the infield unable to advance the runners. Folmar ended the inning stranding both base runners on a long fly to center field.

Americus brought Davenport in to pitch in relief of Williamson in the top of the fifth. Kroh led off for the third time in the game for the Nut Crackers and went out on a grounder to second. Reed hit safely to second, and Holland was also safe on an error by Lindsey. Farmer was up next and lined one to left scoring Reed from second and moving Holland over to third. With the score now 9 to 1, McCullough batted a double to left and pushing Holland and Farmer across the plate increasing the Albany lead to 11 to 1. Mitchell was up next and made it to first on an error by third baseman Williams, but McCullough made out number two going into third. Kimbrell was safe at first on a fielder's choice that failed to get Mitchell out at second. Eldridge made a two-out single to Jackson in right scoring Mitchell from second making the score 12 to 1. Marquardt ended the fun for the visitors on a strike out to pitcher Davenport.

The bottom of the fifth turned out to be the best inning of the game for Americus when three runs were scored. Lindsey led off with a single to left. Duren batted second and went out on a pop up to short. Davenport was safe at first on a fielder's choice that failed to get Lindsey out at second. Nolan was up next and singled on a liner to right moving Davenport to second and scoring Lindsey to make the score 12 to 2. Williams drew a walk as the next batsman loading the bases. Elmore popped up to first for the second out. Jackson came through with a two-out double to center field scoring Davenport and Nolan slightly trimming the Albany lead to 12 to 4. With Jackson at second and Williams at third, Brannan ended the inning with a ground out to short.

All three batters grounded out on the infield for Albany in the top of the sixth. Once again, Kroh had the honors of leading off and went out short to first. Reed grounded out to Nolan at second and Holland copied Kroh grounding out to Lindsey.

Folmar led off the bottom of the sixth with a fly out to left field. Lindsey struck out to follow. Big Bill Parsons pinch hit for Duren and got a single over third. Davenport forced Parsons to be the third out on a fielder's choice to second.

Albany batters went out in order in the top of the seventh. Farmer flew out to center, McCullough grounded out to short, and Mitchell popped up to short.

In the Americus half of the seventh, Nolan led off with a liner to right for a single. Williams batted next and hit what was sure to be a triple or home run to deep center, but Farmer was able to run it down and make an exceptional catch. Nolan had already rounded second and was on his way to third when the ball was caught, and he was unable to make it back to first before being doubled off. Elmore made out number three on a comeback hit to pitcher Kroh who threw on to McCullough at first.

Kimbrell drew a walk to start the top of the eighth for Albany and went to second when Eldridge followed with a base hit to center. Marquardt came up next and was out on a bunt that moved the runners over to second and third. Kroh made the second out going down on strikes. Reed popped up to catcher Barnhart, who came in after Parsons pinch-hit for Duren, for the third out stranding Kimbrell and Eldridge.

Americus batters went one-two-three in the bottom of the inning. Jackson led off flying out to Reed at third. Brannan popped up to third on a bunt attempt for the second out. Folmar was out on a long fly ball to deep right field.

With the game in hand on a comfortable 12 to 4 lead, Albany came to bat in the top of the ninth. Holland hit a liner that was grabbed by shortstop Lindsey for out one. Farmer drew a free pass to first from Davenport. McCullough was almost safe on a low throw to first from Lindsey on a ground ball. Farmer broke for third when Lindsey threw to first and was safe on a wild throw from Brannan. Mitchell ended Albany's batting turn grounding out to short.

Lindsey led off Americus' last chance to salvage the game in the bottom half of the ninth and went down on strikes. Barnhart was also unable to figure out Kroh's slants and whiffed for out number two. Catcher Kimbrell dropped the third strike but was able to throw down to first before Barnhart reached. With two out, Joe Burroughs, pinch-hitting for Davenport, singled to center field. Nolan followed with a single to right, but Burroughs was out at third on a cannon of a throw from Mitchell to end the game 12 to 4.

Bill Nolan led the Americus offense with three hits in five at bats. Joe Jackson got two doubles in four at bats. Buddy Williamson pitched four innings and allowed ten runs on eight hits, four walks, and two strikeouts taking the loss for Americus. Davenport pitched five innings in relief of Williamson allowing two runs on two hits, two walks, and two strikeouts. Kroh got the win for Albany allowing four runs on thirteen hits, three walks, and six strikeouts. Shortstop Johnny Lindsey set what was believed to be a league record making five errors in the game.

The Little World's Series now looked more interesting with Americus leading two games to one over Albany. Game four was scheduled to be played in Albany the following day.

Thursday, August 23, 1923

Americus took game four of the South Georgia league championship series by a 7 to 3 final at the Albany diamond. Things were looking ever more doubtful for Albany in the post-season finals as Americus now had three games and Albany only had one. Initial sacker George Brannan was given credit for winning the game for Americus with his ninth inning two-run homer. Lefty Wingard was also praised for outstanding pitching in relief of Wally Norris.

Americus batted first being the visitors at the Nut Cracker's ball yard with second baseman Bill Nolan going out on a ground ball to pitcher Shaky Kain. Third baseman Bill Williams followed with a single to center and moved over to second on left fielder Verdo Elmore's single through short. Right fielder Joe Jackson batted clean up and advanced Elmore and Williams to second and third on a one-hop out to first unassisted. Shorty Holland fumbled the ball from the bat of first baseman George Brannan allowing Williams and Elmore to score. Albany's Ollie Marquardt threw home trying to head off Elmore, but the throw was late. Brannan cruised into second on the play when catcher Bill Kimbrell couldn't hold on to the ball. With two outs and the score 2 to 0, center fielder Bob Folmar ended the good start for Americus with a soft dribbler to short.

Leading off for Albany in the bottom of the first inning was game one's protested player center fielder George Clarke who went down swinging. Shortstop Harry Holland followed also striking out to the mysterious slants of pitcher Wally Norris. Jack Farmer, who was playing third base, was next with a base hit to right field. Farmer stole second on the first pitch of first baseman Tot McCullough's at bat. McCullough legged out a slow roller to first and Farmer went to third. McCullough stole second without a play due to third base being occupied during the turn of right fielder Orion Mitchell who made the third out short to first.

Shortstop Johnny Lindsey led off the second inning for the visitors hitting a double to left field. Catcher Polly Duren bunted

Lindsey over to third and was out when first baseman McCullough fielded and threw to Marquardt covering first. Pitcher Wally Norris was safe at first on a ground ball to third when Farmer's throw to first went wide pulling McCullough off the bag. Lindsey was unable to score on the play. Nolan walked to fill the bases. Williams came up next and was struck out by Kain. Elmore came through with a big, two-out double to left scoring Lindsey and Norris making the score 4 to 0. Jackson was up next and was intentionally walked. Brannan ended the inning on a fly ball to deep right caught by Mitchell.

Catcher Bill Kimbrell led off the Albany half of the second with a base hit to right, and Milton Reed pinch ran. Americus catcher Duren made a snap throw to first trying to catch Reed off base, and the ball went past Brannan letting Reed get to second. Left fielder Harry Eldridge made the first out on a pop up to third. Second baseman Ollie Marquardt got a clean double to left scoring Reed to make it 4 to 1. Pitcher Shaky Kain grounded to his counterpart Norris who overthrew first affording Marquardt to score and Kain to get to second. Clarke drew a walk from Norris, and Joe Jackson decided to visit his pitcher. Norris, who was a spitball pitcher, told his captain that the balls being put into the game were roughed up and old, not the new, clean balls that were being used at the beginning of the game. Albany knew the spitball artist would need new balls to be effective, so they were exercising their home field advantage and putting old balls into the game. Jackson mentioned to Umpire Erskine Mayer that the balls being put into the game were old and rough and that new balls should be used as much as possible to play a game properly. Mayer refused to give in and said the balls being used were good enough. Norris was losing his control and becoming frustrated, so Jackson stalled as long as Mayer would let him so his pitcher could regain his composure. When play resumed, Holland came to bat flying out to Elmore making a circus catch in left. Farmer ended the inning going out second to first with the score 4 to 2.

Folmar led off the top of the third with a ground out second to first. Lindsey followed with a single to left field and went to third on a wild pitch during Duren's at bat. Duren grounded out to second failing to push Lindsey across. Norris stranded Lindsey by striking out to end the inning.

Albany led off the bottom of the third with McCullough going out on a fly to Elmore in left. Mitchell followed with a solo shot over the left field fence making the score more interesting at 4 to 3. Americus pitcher Norris was still not able to fully effect his spitter on the rough balls, so Jackson, displaying his baseball cleverness, decided to bring in Lefty Wingard to do the hurling. Albany players and fans feared Wingard not only for his excellent pitching but also the wicked willow he swung. Kimbrell came to the plate and hit a slow grounder to first that Brannan couldn't hold on to allowing the batter to be safe. Eldridge batted next and was also safe on an error by Lindsey. Marquardt moved the runners over to second and third on a ground out to short. Shaky Kain ended the inning and left the ducks on the pond fouling out to Duren.

The top of the order came up for Americus in the top of the fourth. Nolan went out on a long fly to right. Williams grounded to short for out number two. Elmore hit safely to left field, but made the third out trying to steal second during Jackson's at bat.

Albany also restarted the batting order in the fourth with Clarke going down on strikes. Duren dropped strike three and threw down to first to get the out. Holland got a free trip to first being hit by a pitch. Farmer was safe at first on a fielder's choice putting Holland out a second. McCullough hit one deep to center field, but it was hauled in by Folmar for out number three.

Joe Jackson led off the top of the fifth for Americus with a ripping single down the first base line. Brannan followed hitting one right to first baseman McCullough who stepped on first and threw to Holland who tagged Jackson out at second completing the double play. Folmar made the third out on a ground ball short to first.

Mitchell started Albany off with a single to left in the bottom of the fifth. Kimbrell followed with a single to right that Jackson let get by him making his only error in an Americus uniform. Mitchell tried to score, but Folmar, backing up Jackson on the play, pegged him out at the plate. The call by Umpire Mayer was argued by Milton Reed as well as all the umpires in the stands, but the call stuck. Kimbrell made it to second on the play but was out at third on another close play when Eldridge hit one to short in the next at bat. Marquardt ended Albany's half of the fifth with a grounder to first unassisted.

Number seven batter Lindsey led off the top of the sixth with a walk. Duren moved him over to second grounding out second to first. Wingard, in his first at bat of the game, struck out to Shaky Kain for out number two. Nolan hit what looked to be a home run, but Mitchell brought it back in against the wall to end the inning.

Still trailing by one with the score 4 to 3, Nut Cracker batters could do no damage in the bottom of the sixth. Kain grounded out to the pitcher, Clarke struck out, and Holland flew out to Elmore in left.

Williams batted first in the Americus half of the seventh and was out grounding to third. Elmore lined one to left and was safe at second when Eldridge dropped the ball. Jackson was walked on purpose with a man in scoring position. Brannan hit what should have been a gapper over short, but left fielder Eldridge made a diving catch for out number two. Elmore and Jackson were stranded on base when Folmar made the third out flying to center.

Albany batters went three up, three down again in the bottom of the seventh. Farmer and McCullough both grounded out third to first, and Mitchell fanned on three nasty pitches from Wingard.

In the top of the eighth inning, Lindsey led off for Americus with a high fly to center field for out one. Duren followed with a foul out to the catcher. Lefty Wingard was safe at first on a line drive to left field and advanced to second on a passed ball. Nolan drew a two-out walk but was stranded with Wingard when Williams made the third out on a fly to right.

Kimbrell went down swinging as the first batter for Albany in the bottom of the eighth. Eldridge came up next and grounded out to second. Marquardt got a clean double lining one to left. Kain left Marquardt out there grounding out second to first to end the inning.

With a 4 to 3 score, Americus went into the top of the ninth needing some insurance since Albany was going to get the last at bat. Verdo Elmore started things off with a single to center field, his fourth hit of the game. Jackson followed with a long single off the right field wall. The insurance Americus needed came from the bat of George Brannan when he hammered the ball out of the park clearing the right field fence by several feet. Three runs scored on the shot to make the score 7 to 3. Folmar batted after Brannan and was the first out flying to right. Lindsey followed with a carbon copy of Folmar's turn. Duren made the third out popping up to the first baseman.

Albany's chances of salvaging the game were much slimmer than they were in the previous inning. Cliff Cameron pinch hit for Clarke and made it safely to second on Lindsey's bad throw to first. Holland was out third to first, and Farmer struck out for outs one and two. McCullough flirted with the fence in Albany's last chance, but Shoeless Joe hauled it in to end the game.

Verdo Elmore had the batting honors going four for five and scoring twice, but George Brannan was called the hero of the game with his ninth inning, three-run home run. Joe Jackson was two for three with two intentional walks, and Johnny Lindsey was two out of four with a double. Wally Norris got the win pitching two and one-third innings and allowing three runs on five hits, one walk, and two strikeouts. Lefty Wingard relieved Norris in the third pitching six and two-thirds innings and allowing no runs on three hits, no free passes, and four strikeouts.

Right fielder Mitchell got the big hit for Albany with a solo home run. Shaky Kain took the loss on the mound pitching the whole game allowing seven runs on twelve hits. He walked five and struck out three.

With game four of the South Georgia league championship series in the bag, Americus now needed only one more win to secure the title. Game five was scheduled for the following day at the Playground diamond.

Friday, August 24, 1923

The South Georgia championship series' game five scheduled to be played at the Playground diamond in Americus was rained out. It was rescheduled for Saturday, August 25.

Saturday, August 25, 1923

Rainfall continued to soak the South Georgia area dampening the hopes of getting game five of the series played at Americus' Playground ball field. Americus was only one win away from taking the title of champion of the circuit over the Nut Crackers of Albany, and now the two teams would have to wait until Monday, August 27 to face off again.

Monday, August 27, 1923

An article appeared in the Americus Times-Recorder newspaper stating that the South Georgia baseball season would be wrapped up today with Americus taking the title. With the blessing of Jupiter Pluvius, the game would be played and won by the home team at the Playground diamond the paper claimed. Sources said that Joe Jackson and his team were anxious to "wind it up" so they could begin a series of exhibition games. The first set of these games scheduled were two against a team from Fitzgerald, Georgia on Tuesday and Wednesday, August 28 and 29. Most of the players on the team would then travel to Bastrop, Louisiana to play a fifteen game schedule where their principle opponent would be the team from Monroe. After the tour of exhibition games, several players, including Jackson and Davenport, were set to return to Americus where they would spend the winter. Jackson had taken out a lease at the Windsor Hotel to run a billiards parlor until next season, and Davenport had secured a position as mechanic in a local garage.

Thinking that the game and the series were in the bag, Americus went into game five with their heads somewhere else besides the field. Albany took the game easily by a 5 to 1 final making the series score three games to two in favor of Americus. The scheduled game with Fitzgerald for Tuesday would now have to wait.

Second baseman Ollie Marquardt led off the game for the visiting Albany Nut Crackers with a fly out to Joe Jackson in center field. Shortstop Harry Holland batted second and fouled out to first baseman George Brannan. First baseman Tot McCullough made the third out on a grounder to second.

Americus came to bat in the bottom of the first leading off second baseman Bill Nolan. Nolan grounded out to his counterpart Marquardt to make the first out. Third baseman Bill Williams was up next and struck out. Left fielder Verdo Elmore ended the inning on a fly out to left.

Right fielder Orion Mitchell led off the second on a pop fly to center field for the first out. Catcher Bill Kimbrell made out number two on a ground ball to first unassisted. Out three came from the bat of left fielder Harry Eldridge flying out to Jackson in center.

Center fielder Joe Jackson led off the bottom of the second for the home team with a ground out short to first. First baseman George Brannan popped up to second, and right fielder Bill Parsons ended the inning on a ground ball to first with the pitcher covering.

Albany sent number seven-hitter center fielder George Clarke to the plate to start the top of the third. He grounded to pitcher Red Hallman who threw on to first. Third baseman Elliott Cooper was up next and flew out to Parsons in right. Pitcher Shaky Kain made the third out of the inning on an unassisted grounder to first.

Shortstop Johnny Lindsey led off the bottom of the third inning with a ground out to the pitcher. Catcher Polly Duren got the first hit of the game on a line drive to center field but was thrown out at second trying to stretch it into a double. Pitcher Red Hallman made out number three on a tap to second.

The top of the order was back for Albany as Marquardt led off the fourth reaching first safely on a booted grounder to short. Holland was up next and went out on a fly ball to left. McCullough came up and was safe at first on a fielder's choice that put Marquardt out at second. Mitchell made the third out on a grounder to Lindsey at short.

Americus also led off the fourth with the top of the batting order as Nolan singled to right. Williams was up next and was struck out by Kain. Elmore came to the plate next and grounded into a four-six-three double play to end the inning.

Kimbrell batted first in the Albany half of the fifth and went out on a fly to right. Eldridge followed and popped up to shallow left. Clarke drew a walk as the next batsman and stole second. Cooper got a double to right and Clarke crossed the plate for the first run of the ball game. Kain ended the inning with a 1 to 0 score going out on a bunt fielded by the catcher.

Jackson led off the one-two-three bottom of the fifth for Americus popping up to second. Brannan did just like Jackson, and Parsons hit a long fly to left for out number three.

The top of the order came back around for Albany in the sixth, and Marquardt led off with a double to left. Holland singled over Williams' head at third, and Marquardt held at third. McCullough followed with a hit to left, and Marquardt and Holland scored to make it 3 to 0. Mitchell came up next and fouled out to catcher Duren. Kimbrell made out two on a slow roller to first. Eldridge flew out to Nolan for the last out.

Shortstop Lindsey led off the Americus half of the sixth with a double to center field. Duren followed with a single over short moving Lindsey over to third. Hallman batted next and lined a single to right easily scoring Lindsey, but Duren went out trying to make it to third. With the score 3 to 1, Nolan one-hopped a hot one to first baseman McCullough who tagged Hallman and stepped on first for the unassisted double play.

Number seven batter Clarke went first in the top of the seventh and grounded short to first for out number one. Cooper hit a long fly ball to deep center, but Shoeless Joe showed the crowd why his glove was known as "the place where triples die" with his famous running, overhead catch. Kain lined one over second for a single but was stranded there when Marquardt struck out.

Americus sent Williams to the plate to lead off the bottom of the seventh. He popped up high to short for the first out. Elmore made out two flying out to Clarke in center. Jackson got a single on a looper to left, but went no further when Brannan grounded out pitcher to first.

The top of the eighth was another prosperous inning for Albany. Holland went to the plate first and was safe at first on a booted grounder to short. McCullough hit a hard double to right, and Holland scored to make it 4 to 1. Mitchell hit one to the wall in left driving McCullough across but was out at the plate trying to stretch it into a round trip. With the score now 5 to 1, Kimbrell hit an easy grounder to the pitcher and was out on the throw to first. Eldridge made the third out on a bunt fielded by catcher Duren.

Time was running out for Americus as the bottom of the eighth rolled around. Big Bill Parsons stepped to the plate to lead off and flew out to center field. Lindsey couldn't catch up to the slants of Kain and fanned. Duren got a single to left, and Hallman followed with a double in the same direction. With Hallman at second and Duren at third, Nolan couldn't capitalize and grounded out second to first.

Clarke led off the top of the last inning with a ground out to short. Cooper came next flying out to Jackson in center. Kain got a two-out single to right but was abandoned there when Marquardt flew out to short.

It was now or never for Americus if Fitzgerald was going to fit into the schedule for tomorrow. Williams stepped up first and flew out to Eldridge in left. Elmore was the second out on an infield fly to short. Jackson doubled to right, but the game was over, 5 to 1, when Brannan popped up to short.

Shaky Kain got the win for Albany pitching all nine innings allowing one run on nine hits, striking out three, and walking none. The losing pitcher was Red Hallman giving up five runs on eight hits, one strikeout, and one base on balls. Polly Duren was perfect at the bat going three for three. Hallman was two for three with a double, and Shoeless Joe Jackson was two for four with a double. Johnny Lindsey got a double and scored the lone run for Americus. Elliott Cooper, Tot McCullough, Ollie Marquardt, and Orion Mitchell all doubled for the Nut Crackers.

The crowd of approximately one thousand saw the Little World's Series become a bit more interesting as Albany now trailed by only one game. Americus would travel to Albany with their three games to two lead for game six the next day hoping to secure the championship.

Tuesday, August 28, 1923

The game Americus had scheduled with Fitzgerald was cancelled in lieu of the necessary game six of the South Georgia Championship series. With a lead of three games to two, Americus needed one more game to secure the title. Hopes of the Americus team were that the series could be wrapped up in this game at the Albany home field. Joe Jackson's gang of ball tossers went into Monday's game with a little too much confidence for their own good and lost the game to Albany. Perhaps this was the wakeup call needed to secure the win of the Little World's Series.

Second baseman Bill Nolan led off for Americus in the top of the first with a double to left field. Third baseman Bill Williams followed and was out on a ground ball to the pitcher that advanced Nolan to third. Left fielder Verdo Elmore fouled one back that was caught by catcher Bill Kimbrell for out two. Clean up man, center fielder Joe Jackson was walked on four straight, very wide pitches. Jackson took the turn toward second after his trot to first drawing a throw from Kimbrell. Nolan sprinted toward home on the throw down, but second baseman Ollie Marquardt threw home instead of tagging Jackson. Nolan saw the throw and tried to retreat to third but was out in a run down.

The Nut Crackers sent second baseman Ollie Marquardt to the plate to lead off the home team half of the first. He was out on a grounder third to first. Shortstop Harry Holland got a single over second. First baseman Tot McCullough was safe on a dribbler to first when Americus first baseman George Brannan fielded and threw wild to second trying to catch Holland on the force. Holland went to third, and McCullough went to second. Right fielder Orion Mitchell popped out to second, and catcher Kimbrell grounded out to first to end the inning.

Right fielder "Big Bill" Parsons led off the top of the second for Americus and was safe on a boot by the shortstop. First baseman George Brannan grounded to the pitcher who threw Parsons out in a force at second. Shortstop Johnny Lindsey batted next and was safe at first on a fielder's choice that forced Brannan out. Catcher Polly Duren made out number three on a foul back to the catcher.

In Albany's half of the second, left fielder Harry Eldridge batted first and was out second to first. Center fielder George Clarke made the second out on a lazy fly ball to short. Third baseman Elliott Cooper ended the inning on a foul fly caught by catcher Duren.

Americus batters also went in order in the top of the third. Pitcher Davenport led off with a slow roller to third for out number one. Nolan was out grounding to first unassisted, and Williams grounded out third to first.

Albany also led off their pitcher in the third inning with Jack Slappey getting a single on a ground ball with eyes past short. Marquardt made the first out striking out to Davenport. The hit and run was on as Holland grounded to the pitcher going out at first advancing Shaky Kain to second running for Slappey. McCullough fouled a high one back that was caught by Duren for the third out.

Elmore came to the plate first in the top of the fourth and was out on a foul fly ball caught by Cooper. Jackson brought the crowd to their feet on a long fly ball to deep center field, but George Clarke hauled it in. Parsons made the last out grounding to first.

Kimbrell batted first for Albany in the fourth frame and flew out to Jackson in shallow center field. Kimbrell lined one to right that looked good for a hit, but Parsons made a diving catch for the out. Eldridge connected well with a pitch from Davenport that bounced off the top of the left field fence and came back into the field for a stand up double. Clarke sent a hot one back to the box that Davenport fielded blindly and threw him out at first to end Albany's turn at bat.

79

In the Americus half of the fifth inning, Brannan led off popping up to Marquardt at second for out one. Lindsey was grazed by an inside pitch and got a free pass. During Duren's at bat, Lindsey stole second. Duren legged one out hit to third, and Lindsey advanced to third. Davenport grounded to the pitcher who threw him out at first. Lindsey tried to score on the play, but McCullough pegged him out on a close play at the plate for the double play.

The bottom of the fifth saw Cooper lead off with a single past first. He would end up stranded there as the next three batters went in order. Slappey grounded out pitcher to first advancing Cooper to second, Marquardt was out grounding to short sending Cooper to third, and Holland lined out to Jackson in center field.

Americus had the big inning in the sixth sending eight men to the plate. Nolan led off with a ground out to second. Williams hit a solo homer over the left field fence to break the ice, 1 to 0. Elmore fanned on the slants of Slappey for the second out. Slappey sent Jackson some chin music in his at bat that hit Jackson sending him to the ground. It was thought that the ball struck Jackson in the head, but it actually hit his hand when he raised it up to protect his head. Nolan took first base to run for Jackson and went to third on a wild pitch during Parsons' at bat. Parsons got a single to right, and Nolan scored Jackson's run making the score 2 to 0 Americus. Slappey threw another wild pitch that allowed Parsons to go to second. Brannan got a single to center field that went through the legs of Clarke and rolled to the wall. Parsons scored to make it 3 to 0, and Brannan went to second standing. Lindsey increased the score to 4 to 0 lining one to center field driving Brannan across. Albany manager Milton Reed decided to make a pitching change at this juncture and brought in Floyd Kroh with one on and two out. Lindsey went to second when Kroh tried to catch him playing off first. "Bunny" also took third on a wild pitch while Duren was at the plate. Duren would be the last batter of the inning for Americus as he was stuck out by Kroh.

Needing to make up some ground on a 4 to 0 trail, Albany came to bat in the bottom of the sixth. McCullough batted first and was out second to first on an easy grounder. Mitchell followed and beat out a single to short. Kimbrell hit one just over shortstop Lindsey's head for a single, and McCullough went to second. Eldridge would have brought rain if it had been a cloudy day with a high fly to the center field fence that was caught by Shoeless Joe. Clarke came up with two outs and ended the inning going down on strikes.

Davenport led off the inning for the second time in the game and was caught looking for the first of what would be three straight outs. Nolan lined a low one to left that was caught by Eldridge on a nice play. Williams grounded out to short.

Third baseman Cooper led off Albany's half of the seventh with a single to left. Kroh batted next and swung hard three times but never connected. Marquardt drew a walk moving Cooper over to second. Holland grounded to Nolan who threw to Lindsey covering second throwing to Brannan for the four-six-three double play.

In the top of the eighth, Elmore led off with a long fly ball to center field that was caught by Clarke. Jackson got a triple to right in his at bat. Parsons followed and flew out to shallow right not deep enough for Jackson to score on the tag. Brannan got a two-out, clutch hit over the middle, and Jackson trotted home to make it 5 to 0. Lindsey ended things for the Americus at bat flying out to center field.

With time running out for Albany, Tot McCullough came up in the bottom of the eighth and was out second to first. Mitchell legged out an easy dribbler down the third base line for a single. Kimbrell was the second out popping up to Williams at third. Eldridge hit one back to pitcher Davenport who, thinking there was only one out, threw to second. Catching Lindsey off guard, he failed to touch the bag before Mitchell got there and both runners were safe. Clarke batted next and one-hopped one to Williams who stepped on third forcing Mitchell out.

Americus batters went one, two, three in the top of the ninth. Duren led off and flew out to right, Davenport popped out to second, and Nolan copied Duren.

Trailing 5 to 0, it was now or never if Albany wanted to force a game seven in the Little World's Series. Joe Jackson sat on the bench and sent Lefty Wingard to play center field for the rest of the game. Cooper led off for Albany with a single to Wingard. Player/manager Milton Reed pinch hit for Kroh and was safe on a fielder's choice that forced Cooper out at second. Marquardt batted next and beat out an infield grounder moving Reed over to second base. Holland lined one over the middle into center, and Reed tried to score from second. Wingard fielded the ball cleanly and came up throwing pegging Reed out at the plate on the fly. McCullough got a two-out single to shallow left that filled the bases. Mitchell stranded all three base runners grounding to Nolan who threw to Lindsey at second forcing McCullough out to end the game and the series.

Davenport got the win for Americus throwing shutout ball on eight hits, one walk, and eight strikeouts. Jack Slappey took the loss for the Nut Crackers giving up four runs in five and two-thirds innings of work. Floyd Kroh allowed the fifth run pitching in relief of Slappey. George Brannan was the only Americus batsman to get more than one hit going two for four. Bill Williams got a home run as his only hit, Joe

Jackson had a triple, and Bill Nolan got a double. Johnny Lindsey had two stolen bases to add to his seven totaled from the regular season.

With the South Georgia championship now in the bag with four wins and two losses, the Americus team could celebrate their victory over long-time rival in many sports, Albany. It was now on to Fitzgerald for two games there, then to Bastrop, Louisiana for a fifteen game schedule before calling it a season.

Most all of the Americus players had strong contributions to the winning of the South Georgia Championship series. Barnhart only got into one game for one at bat, but he capitalized on it with a single. George Brannan played in all six games and hit two home runs. Joe Burroughs only played in one of the games and got a single as a pinch hitter. Davenport pitched in two games winning one and losing none. Polly Duren batted .429 in six games and had a fielding average of 1.000. Verdo Elmore also fielded perfectly across six games and batted a strong .462. Bob Folmar played in four games and played perfect defense. Red Hallman pitched in two games with one win and one loss. Shoeless Joe Jackson played in all six games batting .500 with four doubles, one triple, two home runs, and scoring eight runs. His fielding average was .941 for the series as he made his only error in an Americus uniform in game four. Johnny Lindsey played in all six games and stole two bases in game six. Bill Nolan also appeared in all six games and scored six runs. Wally Norris appeared in only one game pitching for two innings, but it was good enough to get a win. Bill Parsons played in four games and had a fielder average of 1.000. Bill Williams hit three homeruns, two in game two, and scored six runs across the six games he played. Buddy Williamson only appeared in one game for Americus pitching four innings and getting the loss in game three. Lefty Wingard pitched in two games winning one and losing none and played center field for one inning in game six. He batted .714 with one home run and had a fielding average of 1.000 for the series. Although Shoeless Joe was the star attraction of the Americus team, there were quite a few other stars that shown brightly en route to winning the Little World's Series.

Beyond the 1923 Summer

Shoeless Joe Jackson was set to return to Americus to run a billiards hall at the Windsor Hotel for the winter after the short Louisiana tour of games. But his plans changed when an offer from the Waycross team of the Atlantic Coastline railroad circuit came in, and he, along with Lefty Wingard, went there for the rest of the season. Jackson stayed there for the next couple of years. In 1929, he moved back to his home in Greenville, South Carolina where he ran various businesses such as laundry-mats and a liquor store. He also played semi-pro baseball for the next few years and taught children the great game of baseball every chance he got. Shoeless Joe never felt any ill will towards Major League Baseball, and he always professed his innocence in the 1919 World Series scandal. In 1949, in an interview with Furman Bisher of the Atlanta Journal Constitution, Joe told his story for the record to be set straight. He told Bisher "my conscience is clear, and I'll stand on my record in that (1919) World Series. I'm willing to let the Lord be my judge." On December 5, 1951, Shoeless Joe Jackson died of a massive heart attack at his home in Greenville, South Carolina. His final words were "The good Lord will know I'm innocent. Goodbye, good buddy. This is it."

With fifty years passed since the death of Joe Jackson, the time has come for the wrong to be righted. Although two separate courts of law found Shoeless Joe to be innocent of all charges stemmed from the 1919 World Series scandal in two separate trials, Major League Baseball continues to uphold the pompous decision of banishment made by then commissioner Kenesaw Mountain Landis. It was Landis' arrogance that made him ignore the lawful court decision, and his pride that never allowed him to take it back. Today, it has been requested of Major League Baseball time and time again to review the evidence and consider reinstating Joe Jackson making him eligible for the baseball hall of fame. Rather than listening to the masses of people who would like to see Joe take his rightful place at Cooperstown, baseball continues to only hear the opinions of a few who adamantly continue the injustice.

You can help by visiting www.blackbetsy.com and joining the Shoeless Joe Jackson Society. This is an excellent website for any Joe Jackson fan. It has the facts that prove Joe's innocence in the 1919 scandal as well as a lot of interesting information, photos, and links.

There are also instructions on how you can help get Joe reinstated in baseball.

Joe Jackson was one of the greatest, most gifted baseball players ever, and he was an honest, fair man. He was dealt an unfair hand, but he played it with dignity and made the best of it in all that he did. He came to Americus, Georgia in 1923 and helped a struggling, hometown baseball team get back on its feet and win the league title from its chief sports rival. None of the fans really cared what he was accused of or what he did or didn't do. All they knew was that he was the greatest ball player they had ever seen, and for a short time, they could call him their own. When Shoeless Joe Jackson left Americus, he left memories of a hero to a small baseball town – memories of a Shoeless Summer.

1923 South Georgia League Standings

First Half	W	L	Pct.	GB
Albany Nut Crackers	16	8	.667	---
Dawson	14	8	.636	1.0
Arlington Bell Ringers	15	9	.625	1.0
Americus	8	13	.381	6.5
Blakely Hardwood	7	14	.333	7.5
Bainbridge	7	16	.304	8.5

Second Half	W	L	Pct.	GB
Americus	16	5	.762	---
Albany Nut Crackers	13	8	.619	3.0
Bainbridge	9	12	.429	7.0
Blakely Hardwood	8	13	.381	8.0
Arlington Bell Ringers	disbanded before season end.			
Dawson	disbanded before season end.			

League Championship Series: Americus 4 games, Albany 2 games.

1923 Americus Team of the South Georgia baseball league

Left to right: Bill Nolan, Bill Williams, Eddie Wade, Red Hallman, Lefty Wingard, Polly Duren, Shoeless Joe Jackson (not wearing shoes), Bill Parsons, Verdo Elmore, George Brannan, Johnny Lindsey, Davenport, Barnhart, Red Laird, Joe Burroughs

1923 Americus Players' Bios and Stats
Barnhart

Played for Americus June 29 through August 22.
Barnhart previously played for Norman "Kid" Elberfeld's Little Rock Travelers and the Atlanta Crackers in the class A Southern Association. His brother Clyde played nine seasons, 1920-28, with Pittsburgh of the National League in the outfield and at third base.

Hitting Statistics

Year Club	League	G	AB	R	H	2B	3B	HR	SB	AVG
1923 Americus	So. Georgia	28	99	15	32	2	0	0	1	.323
	League Championship	1	1	0	1	0	0	0	0	1.000

Fielding Statistics

Year Club	League	POS	G	PO	A	E	FA	DP
1923 Americus	So. Georgia	C, RF	26	103	14	4	.967	0
	League Championship	C	1	2	0	0	1.000	0

* * * * * * * * * * * * * * * * * * * *

Bassinger, Otis Alvin

Played for Americus June 27 through July 21.
Threw: Left   Batted: Left
Bassinger was from the Texas and the star pitcher of the baseball team at Southern Methodist University in Dallas from 1923 through 1925. He was also the teams captain his senior year. Bassinger graduated with a B.S in Marketing in 1925.

Pitching Statistics

Year Club	League	G	W	L	PCT	IP	H	BB	R	K
1923 Americus	So. Georgia	7	2	4	.333	57	55	10	30	19

Hitting Statistics

Year Club	League	G	AB	R	H	2B	3B	HR	SB	AVG
1923 Americus	So. Georgia	7	24	2	2	1	0	0	0	.083

Fielding Statistics

Year Club	League	POS	G	PO	A	E	FA	DP
1923 Americus	So. Georgia	P	7	7	8	1	.938	0

* * * * * * * * * * * * * * * * * * * *

Bell, Thomas L. "Tom"

Tom Bell was the field manager for Americus team from July 6 through August 20. He managed fourteen games, seven wins and seven losses, before Shoeless Joe Jackson was given the job of captain in charge of players on July 23. Bell was instrumental in organizing the 1923 Americus baseball team in the South Georgia league. He was also responsible for bringing Joe Jackson to Americus to play. After Jackson was named captain of the Americus team, which was virtually the job of field manager, Bell kept his title of manager of the team. He resigned this position and any official connection with the Americus club just before the first game of the league championship series on August 20 over a dispute of who the umpires should be.

* *

Bloodworth, Luther Usrie "Ludy"

Played for Americus August 10 through August 14.

Bloodworth was a star pitcher of the Mercer University baseball team in Macon, Georgia in 1917 and 1918 and captain of the team his senior year in 1918. A native of Haddock, Georgia, Bloodworth was originally asked to organize the players and manage the team for Americus, but he took an offer to pitch for the Arlington team of the South Georgia league. He and Jimmie Clements, another Mercer man who played for Americus the first game of the season, formed an excellent battery for Arlington. For a short time during the 1923 South Georgia season, Bloodworth caused a controversy about his eligibility to be playing in the league. He had originally agreed to play for the Columbia, South Carolina team of the class B South Atlantic League that season, but he never reported to the team. Because of this, J.H. Farrell's office declared him to be ineligible to participate in professional baseball. His eligibility was no longer in question after it was decided that all players in the South Georgia circuit were free agents. After Arlington disbanded with less than two weeks left in the season, Bloodworth came to Americus and pitched in two games for the team.

Pitching Statistics

Year	Club	League	G	W	L	PCT	IP	H	BB	R	K
1919	Columbia	So. Atl.	2								
1923	Arlington	So. Georgia									
	Americus	So. Georgia	2	1	0	1.000	10	5	0	1	9

Hitting Statistics

Year	Club	League	G	AB	R	H	2B	3B	HR	SB	AVG
1919	Columbia	So. Atl.									
1923	Arlington	So. Georgia									
	Americus	So. Georgia	2	4	0	0	0	0	0	0	.000

Fielding Statistics

Year	Club	League	POS	G	PO	A	E	FA	DP
1919	Columbia	So. Atl.	P	2					
1923	Arlington	So. Georgia	P						
	Americus	So. Georgia	P	7	7	8	1	.938	0

Brannan, Otis Owen "George"

Played for Americus July 23 through August 28.
Born: March 13, 1899 in Greenbrier, Arkansas
Died: June 6, 1967 in Little Rock, Arkansas
Threw: Right   Batted: Left
Height: 5' 9"   Weight: 160 lbs.
Brannan was among the players who came to Americus from Bastrop, Louisiana where he had been playing on a team with Joe Jackson. He went by his real name of Otis in Bastrop and everywhere else there is record of him playing, but for some reason unknown, he was called "George" in Americus. Brannan eventually played for the St. Louis Browns of the American League in 1928 and 1929. He also played for various minor league teams in the "organized" leagues until 1941 where he finished his playing days with Lafayette, Louisiana of the Evangeline League.

Hitting Statistics

Year	Club	League	G	AB	R	H	2B	3B	HR	RBI	SB	AVG
1923	Bastrop	Independent										
	Americus	So. Georgia	23	88	13	20	2	1	1		2	.227
	League Championship		6	27	4	6	1	0	2		0	.222
1928	St. Louis	American	135	483	68	118	18	3	10		9	.244
1929	St. Louis	American	23	51	4	15	1	0	1		0	.294
1930	Hollywood	PCL							18	130		.307
1931	Hollywood	PCL							7	85		.283
1932	Hollywood	PCL							17	111		.311
1933	Hollywood	PCL							14	108		.303
1936	Osceola	NE Arkansas							1	19		.391
1938	Hot Springs	Cotton St.							8	72		.325
1939	Clarksdale	Cotton St.							3	59		.306
1940	Lake Charles	Evangeline							3	24		.261
1941	Clarksdale-Marshall	Cotton St.							1	17		.242
	Lafayette	Evangeline							0	0		.500

Fielding Statistics

Year	Club	League	POS	G	PO	A	E	FA	DP
1923	Bastrop	Independent							
	Americus	**So. Georgia**	**1B**	**23**	**224**	**15**	**10**	**.960**	**7**
	League Championship		**1B**	**6**	**55**	**1**	**3**	**.949**	**1**
1928	St. Louis	American	2B	135	272	434	26	.964	74
1929	St. Louis	American	2B	19	31	47	2	.975	6

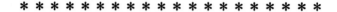

Brown, "Red"

Played for Americus June 25 through July 13.

Hitting Statistics

Year	Club	League	G	AB	R	H	2B	3B	HR	SB	AVG
1923	Americus	So. Georgia	16	65	5	16	1	0	0	0	.246

Fielding Statistics

Year	Club	League	POS	G	PO	A	E	FA	DP
1923	Americus	So. Georgia	LF, RF	16	16	1	4	.810	1

Burroughs, Joe

Played for Americus August 4 through August 22.
Burroughs played for Dawson earlier in the season, but he left soon before the team folded.

Hitting Statistics

Year	Club	League	G	AB	R	H	2B	3B	HR	SB	AVG
1923	Dawson	So. Georgia									
	Americus	**So. Georgia**	**6**	**11**	**3**	**3**	**1**	**0**	**0**	**0**	**.273**
	League Championship		**1**	**1**	**0**	**1**	**0**	**0**	**0**	**0**	**1.000**

Fielding Statistics

Year	Club	League	POS	G	PO	A	E	FA	DP
1923	Dawson	So. Georgia	UT						
	Americus	**So. Georgia**	**UT***	**4**	**10**	**4**	**1**	**.933**	**1**
	League Championship		**PH**						

* Utility Player – played 1B, 2B, 3B, LF, and PH for Americus.

Clements, James Clayton "Jimmie"

Played for Americus June 25.
Clements played baseball at Mercer University in Macon, Georgia from 1914 through 1917 and was captain of the team in 1916. He graduated from Mercer in 1917. Originally from Macon, Georgia, Clements left Americus after playing only one game to play for the Arlington team in the league. He and another Mercer alumnus, Luther Bloodworth, formed an excellent battery for Arlington.

Hitting Statistics

Year Club	League	G	AB	R	H	2B	3B	HR	SB	AVG
1923 Americus	So. Georgia	1	3	1	1	0	0	1	0	.333
Arlington	So. Georgia									

Fielding Statistics

Year Club	League	POS	G	PO	A	E	FA	DP
1923 Americus	So. Georgia	C	1	0	2	0	1.000	0
Arlington	So. Georgia	C, OF						

* * * * * * * * * * * * * * * * * * *

Collier, Paul Arnold "Big Boy"

Played for Americus June 25 through July 21.
Born: April 16, 1899 in Jefferson, Georgia.
Collier played "scrub" baseball at Oglethorpe University in Atlanta, Georgia in 1922.

Hitting Statistics

Year Club	League	G	AB	R	H	2B	3B	HR	SB	AVG
1923 Americus	So. Georgia	23	91	11	30	4	0	0	1	.330

Fielding Statistics

Year Club	League	POS	G	PO	A	E	FA	DP
1923 Americus	So. Georgia	1B	23	250	11	14	.949	5

* * * * * * * * * * * * * * * * * * *

Cox, Pony B.

Played for Americus June 27 through June 29.
Born: November 15, 1903 in Slocumb, Alabama.
Died: September 1985 in Houston, Alabama.
Cox played baseball at Howard College in Birmingham, Alabama only in 1923, his freshman year.

Hitting Statistics

Year Club	League	G	AB	R	H	2B	3B	HR	SB	AVG
1923 Americus	So. Georgia	3	11	2	1	1	0	0	0	.091

Fielding Statistics

Year Club	League	POS	G	PO	A	E	FA	DP
1923 Americus	So. Georgia	C, CF	3	8	0	1	.889	0

* * * * * * * * * * * * * * * * * * * *

Davenport

Played for Americus July 25 through August 28.
Davenport was among the players who came to Americus from Bastrop, Louisiana where he had been playing on a team with Joe Jackson.

Pitching Statistics

Year Club	League	G	W	L	PCT	IP	H	BB	R	K
1923 Bastrop	Independent									
Americus	So. Georgia	7	3	1	.750	40	42	6	18	18
League Championship		2	1	0	1.000	14	15	3	2	5

Hitting Statistics

Year Club	League	G	AB	R	H	2B	3B	HR	SB	AVG
1923 Bastrop	Independent									
Americus	So. Georgia	7	18	1	2	0	0	0	0	.111
League Championship		2	7	1	1	0	0	0	0	.143

Fielding Statistics

Year Club	League	POS	G	PO	A	E	FA	DP
1923 Bastrop	Independent							
Americus	So. Georgia	P	7	0	11	1	.917	1
League Championship		P	2	0	4	0	1.000	0

* * * * * * * * * * * * * * * * * * * *

Dillon

Played for Americus July 20.

Dillon is one of a few "mystery players" whose names appeared in the Americus lineup only on July 20. This date was the first game Shoeless Joe Jackson played in for Americus. It is believed that Dillon was really the regular third baseman Isben "Gid" Wilkes who didn't want to jeopardize his future in the game by playing on the same team as the expelled Jackson.

Hitting Statistics

Year Club	League	G	AB	R	H	2B	3B	HR	SB	AVG
1923 Americus	So. Georgia	1	5	0	1	0	0	0	0	.200

Fielding Statistics

Year Club	League	POS	G	PO	A	E	FA	DP
1923 Americus	So. Georgia	3B	1	0	0	0	.000	0

* * * * * * * * * * * * * * * * * * * *

Dowis, William Herbert "Hub"

Played for Americus June 25 through July 5.

Dowis was a baseball standout at Mercer University in Macon, Georgia in 1916 and 1917, and he also played varsity basketball for the school. Dowis' days in an Americus uniform were cut short on July 5 when news that his brother had been murdered in Duluth, Georgia, his hometown. He left the Americus with intentions of returning but never made it back to rejoin the team.

Hitting Statistics

Year Club	League	G	AB	R	H	2B	3B	HR	SB	AVG
1923 Americus	So. Georgia	10	33	6	7	3	0	0	0	.212

Fielding Statistics

Year Club	League	POS	G	PO	A	E	FA	DP
1923 Americus	So. Georgia	SS, 3B	10	10	20	3	.909	1

* * * * * * * * * * * * * * * * * * * *

Dumas

Played for Americus June 29 through July 21.

Dumas is believed to have played in the July 20 game, the first appearance of Joe Jackson, under the assumed name of "Smith."

Hitting Statistics

Year Club	League	G	AB	R	H	2B	3B	HR	SB	AVG
1923 Americus	So. Georgia	20	76	18	25	2	5	2	5	.329

Fielding Statistics

Year Club	League	POS	G	PO	A	E	FA	DP
1923 Americus	So. Georgia	SS	20	42	54	12	.889	4

* * * * * * * * * * * * * * * * * * * *

Duren, Paul "Polly"

Played for Americus July 23 through August 28.
Duren was among the players who came to Americus from Bastrop, Louisiana where he had been playing on a team with Joe Jackson.

Hitting Statistics

Year Club	League	G	AB	R	H	2B	3B	HR	SB	AVG
1923 Bastrop	Independent									
Americus	So. Georgia	19	67	4	15	4	0	0	0	.224
League Championship		6	21	1	9	1	0	0	0	.429

Fielding Statistics

Year Club	League	POS	G	PO	A	E	FA	DP
1923 Bastrop	Independent							
Americus	So. Georgia	C, LF	19	103	15	0	1.000	2
League Championship		C	6	32	3	0	1.000	0

* * * * * * * * * * * * * * * * * * * *

Elmore, Verdo Wilson, Sr. "Ellie"

Played for Americus July 23 through August 28.
Born: December 10, 1899 in Gordo, Alabama
Died: August 5, 1969 in Birmingham, Alabama
Threw: Right   Batted: Left
Height: 5' 11"   Weight: 185 lbs.
Elmore played for the University of Alabama with Lefty Wingard before joining Joe Jackson's Bastrop, Louisiana team. He came to Americus with other players shortly after Jackson. In 1924, Elmore played for the St. Louis Browns of the American League with Americus and Alabama teammate Lefty Wingard.

Hitting Statistics

Year	Club	League	G	AB	R	H	2B	3B	HR	RBI	SB	AVG
1923	Bastrop	Independent										
	Americus	So. Georgia	19	73	17	27	6	2	0		1	.370
	League Championship		6	26	5	12	1	0	0		0	.462
1924	St. Louis	American	7	17	2	3	3	0	0	0	0	.176

Fielding Statistics

Year	Club	League	POS	G	PO	A	E	FA	DP
1923	Bastrop	Independent							
	Americus	So. Georgia	LF	18	27	4	1	.969	1
	League Championship		LF	6	10	0	0	1.000	0
1924	St. Louis	American	OF	3	0	0	1	.000	0

Folmar, Bob

Played for Americus August 13 through August 23.

Folmar played for the Arlington until the team disbanded at which time he joined the Americus club. He made an excellent addition to the Americus outfield.

Hitting Statistics

Year	Club	League	G	AB	R	H	2B	3B	HR	SB	AVG
1923	Arlington	So. Georgia									
	Americus	So. Georgia	5	15	6	5	0	1	0	1	.333
	League Championship		4	17	3	2	0	0	0	0	.118

Fielding Statistics

Year	Club	League	POS	G	PO	A	E	FA	DP
1923	Arlington	So. Georgia							
	Americus	So. Georgia	CF	5	6	0	0	1.000	0
	League Championship		CF	4	6	1	0	1.000	0

Giddens

Played for Americus July 21.

Giddens is one of the "mystery players" as his name only appeared in the second appearance of Shoeless Joe Jackson for Americus. It is thought that he was really regular third baseman Isben "Gid" Wilkes whose middle name was "Giddens." Wilkes is said to have also played the previous day's game under the name of "Dillon."

Hitting Statistics

Year	Club	League	G	AB	R	H	2B	3B	HR	SB	AVG
1923	Americus	So. Georgia	1	5	2	3	1	0	0	0	.600

Fielding Statistics

Year	Club	League	POS	G	PO	A	E	FA	DP
1923	Americus	So. Georgia	3B	1	0	2	2	.500	0

* * * * * * * * * * * * * * * * * * * *

Hallman, Red

Played for Americus July 24 through August 27.
Hallman was among the players who came to Americus from Bastrop, Louisiana where
he had been playing on a team with Joe Jackson.

Pitching Statistics

Year Club	League	G	W	L	PCT	IP	H	BB	R	K
1923 Bastrop	Independent									
Americus	So. Georgia	8	5	2	.714	62	48	9	17	45
	League Championship	2	1	1	.500	18	13	3	6	8

Hitting Statistics

Year Club	League	G	AB	R	H	2B	3B	HR	SB	AVG
1923 Bastrop	Independent									
Americus	So. Georgia	8	2	1	3	0	0	0	0	.125
	League Championship	2	6	0	2	1	0	0	0	.333

Fielding Statistics

Year Club	League	POS	G	PO	A	E	FA	DP
1923 Bastrop	Independent							
Americus	So. Georgia	P	8	0	10	0	1.000	0
	League Championship	P	2	1	2	0	1.000	0

* * * * * * * * * * * * * * * * * * *

Hogg, Bradley

Played for Americus June 28.
Hogg was field manager for Americus June 25 through July 5. He managed ten games,
three wins, six losses, one tie, and pitched one inning for the team. Hogg was one of the
key figures in organizing the Americus baseball team. He resigned as manager of the
team on July 5 and was replaced by Tom Bell.

Pitching Statistics

Year Club	League	G	W	L	PCT	IP	H	BB	R	K
1923 Americus	So. Georgia	1	0	0	.000	1	3	1	4	0

Hitting Statistics

Year Club	League	G	AB	R	H	2B	3B	HR	SB	AVG
1923 Americus	So. Georgia	1	0	0	0	0	0	0	0	.000

Fielding Statistics

Year Club	League	POS	G	PO	A	E	FA	DP
1923 Americus	So. Georgia	P	1	0	2	0	1.000	0

* * * * * * * * * * * * * * * * * * *

Jackson, Joseph Jefferson "Shoeless Joe"

Played for Americus July 20 through August 28.
Captain for Americus July 23 through August 28.
Games "captained": 31, twenty-two wins, seven losses, and two ties.
Born: July 16, 1889 in Pickens County, South Carolina
Died: December 5, 1951 in Greenville, South Carolina
Threw: Right   Batted: Left
Height: 6' 1"   Weight: 200 lbs.

Jackson was signed to play for Americus by manager Tom Bell. Jackson had just previously been playing and managing a team in Bastrop, Louisiana. After Jackson came to Americus, many players from the Bastrop team followed him. Jackson was named team captain in charge of players on July 23 and led the Americus squad to twenty-two wins, seven losses, and two ties under his leadership. This record won the second half of the season for Americus and a spot to face Albany in the South Georgia league championship series. Americus won the series behind Jackson four games to two. After the season, Jackson, along with pitcher Ernest "Lefty" Wingard, went to play and manage a team in Waycross, Georgia.

Pitching Statistics

Year Club	League	G	W	L	PCT	IP	H	BB	R	K
1923 Americus	So. Georgia	1	0	0	.000	1	0	1	0	0

Hitting Statistics

Year Club	League	G	AB	R	H	2B	3B	HR	RBI	SB	AVG
1908 Philadelphia	American	5	23	0	3	0	0	0	3	0	.130
1909 Philadelphia	American	5	17	3	3	0	0	0	0	0	.176
1910 Cleveland	American	20	75	15	29	2	5	1	11	4	.387
1911 Cleveland	American	147	571	126	233	45	19	7	83	41	.408
1912 Cleveland	American	152	572	121	226	44	26	3	90	35	.395
1913 Cleveland	American	148	528	109	197	39	17	7	71	26	.373
1914 Cleveland	American	122	453	61	153	22	13	3	53	22	.338
1915 Cleveland	American	83	303	42	99	16	9	3	45	10	.327
Chicago	American	45	158	21	43	4	5	2	36	6	.272
1916 Chicago	American	155	592	91	202	40	21	3	78	24	.341
1917 Chicago	American	146	538	91	162	20	17	5	75	13	.301
1918 Chicago	American	17	65	9	23	2	2	1	20	3	.354
1919 Chicago	American	139	516	79	181	31	14	7	96	9	.351
1920 Chicago	American	146	570	105	218	42	20	12	121	9	.382
1923 Bastrop	Independent	29	96	27	28			4			.396
Americus	**So. Georgia**	**25**	**86**	**25**	**39**	**10**	**2**	**5**		**0**	**.453**
League Championship		**6**	**22**	**8**	**11**	**4**	**1**	**2**		**0**	**.500**
Waycross	Atl. Coastline RR										
1924 Waycross	Atl. Coastline RR										
1925 Waycross	Atl. Coastline RR										

Fielding Statistics

Year Club	League	POS	G	PO	A	E	FA	DP
1908 Philadelphia	American	OF	5	6	1	1	.875	0
1909 Philadelphia	American	OF	4	10	0	2	.833	0
1910 Cleveland	American	OF	20	40	2	1	.977	0
1911 Cleveland	American	OF	147	242	32	12	.958	8
1912 Cleveland	American	OF	150	273	30	16	.950	2
1913 Cleveland	American	OF	148	211	28	18	.930	5
1914 Cleveland	American	OF	119	195	13	7	.967	4
1915 Cleveland	American	OF, 1B	79	352	21	10	.974	12
Chicago	American	OF	46	84	6	5	.947	1

1916	Chicago	American	OF		155	290	17	8	.975	5
1917	Chicago	American	OF		145	341	18	6	.984	4
1918	Chicago	American	OF		17	36	1	0	1.000	0
1919	Chicago	American	OF		139	252	15	9	.967	4
1920	Chicago	American	OF		145	314	14	12	.965	2
1923	Bastrop	Independent	OF							
	Americus	So. Georgia	LF, CF, RF, P		25	26	2	0	1.000	1
	League Championship		CF, RF		6	16	0	1	.941	0

Jones

Played for Americus July 20.

Jones is another one of the "mystery players" whose names appeared in the Americus line-up only on July 20. It is believed that he was really the regular center fielder Eddie Wade who was unsure if his name would be tainted by playing with Joe Jackson. Wade's name reappeared in the lineup on July 21 when these fears were put to rest.

Hitting Statistics

Year	Club	League	G	AB	R	H	2B	3B	HR	SB	AVG
1923	Americus	So. Georgia	1	5	2	1	0	0	0	0	.200

Fielding Statistics

Year	Club	League	POS	G	PO	A	E	FA	DP
1923	Americus	So. Georgia	CF	1	4	0	0	1.000	0

Laird, Green Flake "Red"

Played for Americus June 25 through August 6.

Hailing from Decatur, Georgia, Laird was the star pitcher of the University High baseball team. He also won eight and lost zero games for Davidson College in Davidson, North Carolina during the spring of 1923. He played varsity baseball, football, and basketball for Davidson and graduated in 1926.

Pitching Statistics

Year	Club	League	G	W	L	PCT	IP	H	BB	R	K
1923	Americus	So. Georgia	12	4	2	.667	77	69	21	36	31

Hitting Statistics

Year	Club	League	G	AB	R	H	2B	3B	HR	SB	AVG
1923	Americus	So. Georgia	14	37	3	3	0	0	0	0	.081

Fielding Statistics

Year	Club	League	POS	G	PO	A	E	FA	DP
1923	Americus	So. Georgia	P, 2B, LF, CF	14	10	15	0	1.000	0

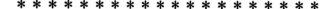

Lindsey, Johnny S. "Bunny"

Played for Americus July 23 through August 28.
Lindsey was among the players who came to Americus from Bastrop, Louisiana where he
had been playing on a team with Joe Jackson.

Hitting Statistics

Year Club	League	G	AB	R	H	2B	3B	HR	SB	AVG
1923 Bastrop	Independent									
Americus	So. Georgia	23	84	22	27	4	0	1	7	.321
League Championship		6	21	6	7	2	0	0	2	.333

Fielding Statistics

Year Club	League	POS	G	PO	A	E	FA	DP
1923 Bastrop	Independent							
Americus	So. Georgia	SS	23	62	60	12	.910	6
League Championship		SS	6	19	16	11	.761	1

* *

McClelland

Played for Americus July 19 through July 20.

Hitting Statistics

Year Club	League	G	AB	R	H	2B	3B	HR	SB	AVG
1923 Americus	So. Georgia	2	8	0	0	0	0	0	0	.000

Fielding Statistics

Year Club	League	POS	G	PO	A	E	FA	DP
1923 Americus	So. Georgia	C, 2B	2	4	4	1	.889	0

* *

Motts

Played for Americus August 10.

Pitching Statistics

Year Club	League	G	W	L	PCT	IP	H	BB	R	K
1923 Americus	So. Georgia	1	0	0	.000	7	7	5	5	4

Hitting Statistics

Year Club	League	G	AB	R	H	2B	3B	HR	SB	AVG
1923 Americus	So. Georgia	1	3	1	1	0	0	0	0	.333

Fielding Statistics

Year Club	League	POS	G	PO	A	E	FA	DP
1923 Americus	So. Georgia	P	1	0	0	0	.000	0

* *

Nolan, Bill

Played for Americus July 23 through August 28.
Nolan was among the players who came to Americus from Bastrop, Louisiana where he had been playing on a team with Joe Jackson. He was originally from Oakridge, Louisiana.

Hitting Statistics

Year	Club	League	G	AB	R	H	2B	3B	HR	SB	AVG
1923	Bastrop	Independent									
	Americus	So. Georgia	23	94	20	19	4	0	0	1	.202
	League Championship		6	27	2	7	1	1	0	0	.259

Fielding Statistics

Year	Club	League	POS	G	PO	A	E	FA	DP
1923	Bastrop	Independent							
	Americus	So. Georgia	2B	23	67	75	7	.953	4
	League Championship		2B	6	15	16	1	.969	1

* *

Norris, Wally

Played for Americus August 13 through August 23.
Norris pitched for Arlington until the team disbanded late in the season at which time he joined the Americus team.

Pitching Statistics

Year	Club	League	G	W	L	PCT	IP	H	BB	R	K
1923	Albany	So. Georgia									
	Arlington	So. Georgia									
	Americus	So. Georgia	2	1	1	.500	11	11	4	5	7
	League Championship		1	1	0	1.000	2	5	1	3	2

Hitting Statistics

Year	Club	League	G	AB	R	H	2B	3B	HR	SB	AVG
1923	Albany	So. Georgia									
	Arlington	So. Georgia									
	Americus	So. Georgia	2	6	0	3	2	0	0	0	.500
	League Championship		1	2	1	1	0	0	0	0	.500

Fielding Statistics

Year	Club	League	POS	G	PO	A	E	FA	DP
1923	Albany	So. Georgia	P						
	Arlington	So. Georgia	P						
	Americus	So. Georgia	P	2	0	4	0	1.000	0
	League Championship		P	1	0	0	1	.000	0

* *

Overstreet, Morris

Played for Americus June 28 through June 30.
Overstreet was a native of Hahira, Georgia.

Pitching Statistics

Year Club	League	G	W	L	PCT	IP	H	BB	R	K
1923 Americus	So. Georgia	2	0	1	.000	10	13	4	15	1
Dawson	So. Georgia									

Hitting Statistics

Year Club	League	G	AB	R	H	2B	3B	HR	SB	AVG
1923 Americus	So. Georgia	2	3	0	0	0	0	0	0	.000
Dawson	So. Georgia									

Fielding Statistics

Year Club	League	POS	G	PO	A	E	FA	DP
1923 Americus	So. Georgia	P	2	0	2	1	.667	0
Dawson	So. Georgia							

* * * * * * * * * * * * * * * * * * *

Owens, Lefty

Played for Americus June 28 through July 20.
Threw: Left   Batted: Left

Pitching Statistics

Year Club	League	G	W	L	PCT	IP	H	BB	R	K
1923 Americus	So. Georgia	7	2	3	.400	43	37	7	21	13

Hitting Statistics

Year Club	League	G	AB	R	H	2B	3B	HR	SB	AVG
1923 Americus	So. Georgia	7	12	2	1	0	0	0	0	.083

Fielding Statistics

Year Club	League	POS	G	PO	A	E	FA	DP
1923 Americus	So. Georgia	P	7	0	7	0	1.000	0

* * * * * * * * * * * * * * * * * * *

Pantone, Clifford M. "Cliff"

Played for Americus June 27.
Pantone played baseball for the University of Georgia in Athens from 1921 through 1923.

Hitting Statistics

Year Club	League	G	AB	R	H	2B	3B	HR	SB	AVG
1923 Americus	So. Georgia	1	4	0	2	1	0	0	0	.500

Fielding Statistics

Year Club	League	POS	G	PO	A	E	FA	DP
1923 Americus	So. Georgia	CF	1	1	1	0	1.000	0

* * * * * * * * * * * * * * * * * * *

Parker, Jasper "Jap"

Played for Americus June 25.
Parker played baseball for Americus High School in 1922 and 1923.

Hitting Statistics

Year Club	League	G	AB	R	H	2B	3B	HR	SB	AVG
1923 Americus	So. Georgia	1	3	0	1	0	0	0	0	.333

Fielding Statistics

Year Club	League	POS	G	PO	A	E	FA	DP
1923 Americus	So. Georgia	CF	1	4	0	0	1.000	0

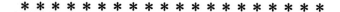

Parsons, Bill "Big Bill"

Played for Americus June 25 through August 28.
Hailing from Americus, Parsons was the only player to be in the Americus lineup on the first official game of the season all the way through to the last game of the championship series. Parsons had previously played industrial league baseball in the Americus area for the Southerfield team.

Pitching Statistics

Year Club	League	G	W	L	PCT	IP	H	BB	R	K
1923 Americus	So. Georgia	1	0	0	.000	4	5	7	5	3

Hitting Statistics

Year Club	League	G	AB	R	H	2B	3B	HR	SB	AVG
1923 Americus	So. Georgia	26	86	8	29	9	0	0	0	.337
	League Championship	4	8	1	2	0	0	0	0	.250

Fielding Statistics

Year Club	League	POS	G	PO	A	E	FA	DP
1923 Americus	So. Georgia	RF, LF, P	24	33	4	3	.925	0
	League Championship	RF	3	3	0	0	1.000	0

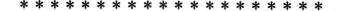

Paul

Played for Americus July 4 through July 27.
Paul previously pitched in the Savannah city league.

Pitching Statistics

Year Club	League	G	W	L	PCT	IP	H	BB	R	K
1923 Americus	So. Georgia	5	0	3	.000	31	25	12	19	12

Hitting Statistics

Year Club	League	G	AB	R	H	2B	3B	HR	SB	AVG
1923 Americus	So. Georgia	15	51	10	14	5	0	0	0	.275

Fielding Statistics

Year Club	League	POS	G	PO	A	E	FA	DP
1923 Americus	So. Georgia	P, RF, LF	15	10	12	4	.846	0

Pinkston

Played for Americus June 25 through July 19.

After the first half of the season, Pinkston went to play for Arlington possibly fearing for his eligibility if he played on the same team as Joe Jackson.

Hitting Statistics

Year Club	League	G	AB	R	H	2B	3B	HR	SB	AVG
1923 Americus	So. Georgia	22	83	12	14	1	0	0	1	.169
Arlington	So. Georgia									

Fielding Statistics

Year Club	League	POS	G	PO	A	E	FA	DP
1923 Americus	So. Georgia	2B	22	49	68	6	.951	6
Arlington	So. Georgia							

Player, Edwin

Played for Americus June 28.

An Americus local, Player was a standout on the Americus High School baseball from 1921 through 1923. He was also captain of the team in 1923, his year of graduation.

Hitting Statistics

Year Club	League	G	AB	R	H	2B	3B	HR	SB	AVG
1923 Americus	So. Georgia	1	3	1	2	0	0	0	0	.667

Fielding Statistics

Year Club	League	POS	G	PO	A	E	FA	DP
1923 Americus	So. Georgia	RF	1	0	1	0	1.000	0

Randolph

Played for Americus July 21.

Randolph is considered to be one of the "mystery players" as his name only appeared in the second appearance of Shoeless Joe for Americus. It is thought that he was really Pinkston who was not in the lineup for the first game of Jackson's play in Americus.

Hitting Statistics

Year Club	League	G	AB	R	H	2B	3B	HR	SB	AVG
1923 Americus	So. Georgia	1	5	0	3	0	0	0	0	.600

Fielding Statistics

Year Club	League	POS	G	PO	A	E	FA	DP
1923 Americus	So. Georgia	2B	1	5	4	0	1.000	0

Smith

Played for Americus July 20.

Smith is one of the "mystery players" whose names appeared in the Americus line-up only on July 20. He was believed to actually be the regular shortstop Dumas who was unsure about his future in the game if he played with Joe Jackson.

Hitting Statistics

Year Club	League	G	AB	R	H	2B	3B	HR	SB	AVG
1923 Americus	So. Georgia	1	5	2	3	0	0	0	0	.600

Fielding Statistics

Year Club	League	POS	G	PO	A	E	FA	DP
1923 Americus	So. Georgia	SS	1	5	1	0	1.000	0

Spikes

Played for Americus June 30 through July 3.

Hitting Statistics

Year Club	League	G	AB	R	H	2B	3B	HR	SB	AVG
1923 Americus	So. Georgia	3	13	0	2	0	0	0	0	.154

Fielding Statistics

Year Club	League	POS	G	PO	A	E	FA	DP
1923 Americus	So. Georgia	CF, RF	3	11	0	1	.917	0

* *

Wade, Eddie

Played for Americus July 3 through August 10.

Hailing from Parrott, Georgia, Wade is believed to have played in the July 20 game, the first appearance of Joe Jackson, under the assumed name of "Jones." His name was back in the lineup for the next game on July 21.

Hitting Statistics

Year Club	League	G	AB	R	H	2B	3B	HR	SB	AVG
1923 Americus	So. Georgia	28	105	16	22	5	0	3	2	.210

Fielding Statistics

Year Club	League	POS	G	PO	A	E	FA	DP
1923 Americus	So. Georgia	CF, LF	28	66	1	6	.918	0

* * * * * * * * * * * * * * * * * * * *

Walton

Played for Americus July 18 through July 21.

Hitting Statistics

Year Club	League	G	AB	R	H	2B	3B	HR	SB	AVG
1923 Americus	So. Georgia	3	7	3	4	0	0	0	0	.571

Fielding Statistics

Year Club	League	POS	G	PO	A	E	FA	DP
1923 Americus	So. Georgia	C, 1B	3	6	2	0	1.000	0

* * * * * * * * * * * * * * * * * * * *

Wilkes, Isben Giddens "Gid"

Played for Americus June 27 through July 19.

Wilkes was called one of the fastest infielders in baseball during the time he played in Americus. Hailing from Adel, Georgia, he played varsity baseball for Mercer University from 1921 through 1923, and was also a member of the varsity basketball team. Wilkes is believed to have played in the July 20 game, the first appearance of Joe Jackson, under the assumed name of "Dillon" as he was unsure how being in the lineup with the expelled player would affect his future. In the July 21 game, he also is believed to have played under the name of "Giddens." He went to play for the Blakely team of the South Georgia league at the end of the first half of the season.

Hitting Statistics

Year	Club	League	G	AB	R	H	2B	3B	HR	SB	AVG
1923	Americus	So. Georgia	15	60	8	13	1	2	0	1	.217
	Blakely	So. Georgia									

Fielding Statistics

Year	Club	League	POS	G	PO	A	E	FA	DP
1923	Americus	So. Georgia	3B	15	12	24	8	.818	0
	Blakely	So. Georgia	3B, SS						

* *

Williams, Bill

Played for Americus July 23 through August 28.
Williams was among the players who came to Americus from Bastrop, Louisiana where he had been playing on a team with Joe Jackson. He played baseball for Louisiana Tech in 1922.

Hitting Statistics

Year	Club	League	G	AB	R	H	2B	3B	HR	SB	AVG
1923	Bastrop	Independent									
	Americus	So. Georgia	23	95	25	31	11	1	1	0	.326
	League Championship		6	27	6	7	0	0	3	0	.259

Fielding Statistics

Year	Club	League	POS	G	PO	A	E	FA	DP
1923	Bastrop	Independent								
	Americus	So. Georgia	3B	23	17	33	8	.862	3
	League Championship		3B	6	7	6	2	.867	0

* *

Williamson, Buddy

Played for Americus August 22.
Williamson came from Blakely where he pitched in the regular season. Although on the roster for the last week of the regular season, he only played for Americus during the championship series.

Pitching Statistics

Year	Club	League	G	W	L	PCT	IP	H	BB	R	K
1923	Blakely	So. Georgia									
	Americus	So. Georgia									
	League Championship		1	0	1	.000	4	8	5	10	0

Hitting Statistics

Year	Club	League	G	AB	R	H	2B	3B	HR	SB	AVG
1923	Blakely	So. Georgia									
	Americus	So. Georgia									
	League Championship		1	1	0	0	0	0	0	0	.000

Fielding Statistics

Year	Club	League	POS	G	PO	A	E	FA	DP
1923	Blakely								
	Americus	So. Georgia							
	League Championship		P	1	0	1	1	.500	0

* *

Wingard, Ernest James, Sr. "Lefty"

Played for Americus July 23 through August 28.
Born: October 17, 1900 in Prattville, Alabama
Died: January 17, 1977 in Prattville, Alabama
Threw: Left   Batted: Left
Height: 6' 2"   Weight: 176 lbs.
Wingard came to Americus with Jackson from Bastrop, Louisiana. He had formerly pitched for the University of Alabama where he played with Verdo Elmore. Wingard pitched the next season, 1924, for the St. Louis Brown in the American League and stayed there until 1927. He was joined, in 1924, by Americus and U. of A. teammate Verdo Elmore on the Browns team. He played successfully in organized baseball until 1941 despite his association with Shoeless Joe Jackson. Late in his career, he lost his ability to pitch effectively, but his solid batting skills kept him in the game as a first baseman. He is credited with hitting 150 home runs during his career in organized baseball in the major and minor leagues. Wingard ended his playing career with Thomasville of the Georgia-Florida League, ironically, playing against Americus in the same league. Wingard's son, Ernest, Jr., also played in the minor leagues from 1949 through 1953.

Pitching Statistics

Year	Club	League	G	W	L	PCT	ERA	IP	H	BB	R	K
1923	Bastrop	Independent										
	Americus	So. Georgia	8	5	1	.833		56	51	11	28	37
	League Championship		2	1	0	1.000		15	7	2	4	9
1924	St. Louis	American	36	13	12	.520	3.51	218	215	85	103	23
1925	St. Louis	American	32	9	10	.474	5.52	145	183	77	111	20
1926	St. Louis	American	39	5	8	.385	3.57	169	188	76	86	30
1927	St. Louis	American	38	2	13	.133	6.56	156	213	79	132	28
1930	Toledo	AA		8	7	.533	4.34					
1931	Toledo	AA		7	7	.500	5.34					
1932	Indianapolis	AA		7	7	.500						
1933	Indianapolis	AA		0	0		9.00					
1934	Milwaukee	AA		1	5	.166	5.56					
1938	Dothan	Ala.-Fla.	13	2	2	.500	5.14	49	56	10	30	21
1939	Dothan	Ala.-Fla.										

Hitting Statistics

Year	Club	League	G	AB	R	H	2B	3B	HR	RBI	SB	AVG
1923	Bastrop	Independent										
	Americus	**So. Georgia**	**8**	**25**	**4**	**5**	**1**	**0**	**1**		**0**	**.200**
	League Championship		**3**	**7**	**3**	**5**	**0**	**0**	**1**		**0**	**.714**
1924	St. Louis	American	37	77	8	18	1	1	3	10	0	.234
1925	St. Louis	American	34	52	12	15	2	2	1	11	0	.288
1926	St. Louis	American	42	61	4	14	4	0	0	5	0	.230
1927	St. Louis	American	42	56	6	10	2	1	3	12	0	.179
1930	Toledo	AA							24	104		.342
1931	Toledo	AA							18	98		.306
1932	Indianapolis	AA							13	75		.343
1933	Indianapolis	AA							8	84		.296
1934	Ind.-Milwaukee	AA							8	67		.291
1935	Mil.-Toledo	AA							7	71		.289
1936	Troy	Ala.-Fla.	105	421	73	128	24	2	14	90	5	.328
1938	Dothan	Ala.-Fla.	128	499	96	178	25	9	10	100	11	.357
1939	Dothan	Ala.-Fla.	127	501	102	180	34	14	18	137	11	.359
1940	Tallassee	Alabama St.	36	156	30	53	9	3	9	42	1	.340
1941	Thomasville	Ga.-Fla.	34	96	13	26	3	0	2	15	0	.271

Fielding Statistics

Year	Club	League	POS	G	PO	A	E	FA	DP
1923	Bastrop	Independent	P						
	Americus	**So. Georgia**	**P**	**8**	**5**	**19**	**0**	**1.000**	**1**
	League Championship		**P, CF**	**3**	**0**	**6**	**0**	**1.000**	**0**
1924	St. Louis	American	P	36	10	42	3	.945	1
1925	St. Louis	American	P	32	6	49	5	.917	3
1926	St. Louis	American	P	39	10	58	3	.958	3
1927	St. Louis	American	P	35	14	45	3	.952	1
1936	Troy	Ala.-Fla.	1B	105	979	47	9	.991	77
1938	Dothan	Ala.-Fla.	P, 1B	124	1055	34	15	.986	71
1939	Dothan	Ala.-Fla.	P, 1B	127	1100	31	21	.982	88
1940	Tallassee	Alabama St.	1B	36	340	11	1	.997	20
1941	Thomasville	Ga.-Fla.	1B	34	254	9	10	.964	18

* *

Wright, Howard

Played for Americus July 9 through July 10.

Originally from Eastman, Georgia, Wright came to Americus being called one of the best catchers in the state of Georgia. He had previously played in Valdosta and Waycross of the Georgia State League and had managed the Spartanburg, South Carolina team in the South Atlantic League.

Hitting Statistics

Year	Club	League	G	AB	R	H	2B	3B	HR	SB	AVG
1923	Americus	So. Georgia	2	5	0	1	0	0	0	0	.200

Fielding Statistics

Year	Club	League	POS	G	PO	A	E	FA	DP
1923	Americus	So. Georgia	C	8	5	19	0	1.000	1

South Georgia League Players
<u>Name – Team(s) Played For – Position(s) Played</u>

Adams – Arlington – 1B
Angel, Louis – Albany – C
Angley – Bainbridge – OF
Arnold – Bainbridge – SS
Austin, Pete – Albany, Blakely – 2B, OF
Barnhart – Americus – C, OF
Bassinger, Otis Alvin – Americus – P
Bloodworth, Luther Usrie "Ludy" – Arlington, Americus - P
Boney, Sam – Albany
Bostwick, R.H. "Bob" – Arlington – 1B
Brannan, Otis Owen "George" – Americus – 1B
Brown, Red – Americus – OF
Brunner – Dawson – SS
Burroughs, Joe – Dawson, Americus – 1B, 3B, UT
Bush – Bainbridge – 3B
Cameron, Cliff – Albany – 2B, OF
Camp, Cliff – Albany – P
Cassares – Dawson – P
Clarke, George – Blakely, Albany – OF, P
Clements, James Clayton "Jimmie" – Americus, Arlington – C, OF
Cochran, Alvah Jackson "Goat" – Blakely, Albany – P, 3B
Collier, Paul Arnold "Big Boy" – Americus – 1B
Conway – Blakely – SS, OF
Cooper, Elliott – Albany – 3B
Cordell, Al – Bainbridge – P
Cosby – Dawson – P
Cox, Pony B. – Americus – C, OF
Daniels – Dawson – OF
Davenport – Americus – P
Davis – Arlington – SS
Dillon (Gid Wilkes) – Americus – 3B
Dowis – Bainbridge – P
Dowis – William Herbert "Hub" – Americus – SS, 3B
Dozier – Arlington – 2B
Dumas – Americus – SS
Duren – Paul "Polly" – Americus – C, OF
Dutto – Bainbridge – OF
Eady, Chick – Albany – P
Edwards – Blakely – 1B
Eldridge, Harry "Old-Timer" – Albany – 1B, OF
Ellis, Bill – Blakely, Albany – P
Elmore, Verdo Wilson, Sr. "Ellie" – Americus – OF
Farmer, Jack – Albany – OF
Farrer, Greene – Albany – P, OF
Fincher – Blakely – C, 3B
Folmar, Bob – Arlington, Americus – OF
Gibson, Charlie – Bainbridge – C
Giddens (Gid Wilkes) – Americus – 3B
Graybill – Arlington – OF
Haefer – Bainbridge – SS
Hallman, Red – Americus – P

Hamilton – Bainbridge – P
Harmon – Bainbridge – 2B
Harrell – Bainbridge – OF
Hecker – Bainbridge – P
Henderson, Hap – Blakely, Dawson – P, OF
Hicks (Bill Statham) – Albany – P
Hines, Emmett – Dawson – P, OF
Hodges, Charlie – Albany, Arlington – 2B
Hogg, Bradley – Americus – P
Holland, Harry – Albany – SS, 3B
Holland, Jack – Arlington – P
Hollingsworth – Blakely – P
Hope – Blakely – SS
Jackson, Joseph Jefferson "Shoeless Joe" – Americus – OF, P
Jenkins, Roy – Blakely – OF
Jones – Dawson
Jones (Eddie Wade) – Americus – OF
Kain, Shaky – Albany – P, OF
Kamisky – Dawson – 3B
Kimbrell, Bill – Albany – C
Knowles – Bainbridge – 1B
Koenigsmark, William Thomas "Will" – Arlington – P
Konneman – Bainbridge – P
Kroh, Floyd Myron "Rube" – Albany – P
Laing – Blakely – P
Laird, Green Flake "Red" – Americus – P, 2B, OF
Lawrence – Arlington – OF, C
Lawrence – Dawson – 2B
Lightfoot – Dawson – 1B, C
Lightfoot, Bob – Arlington – 2B
Liles – Blakely – P
Lindsey, Johnny S. "Bunny" – Americus – SS
Long – Bainbridge – P
Lowery, Dick – Blakely – P, OF
Lucas, Grunt – Dawson – P
Mannion – Dawson – 3B
Marquardt, Albert Ludwig "Ollie" – Dawson, Albany – 2B, 3B
McClelland – Americus – C, 2B
McCullough, Carl – Albany – OF
McCullough, Tot – Albany – 1B
McKenzie – Bainbridge – OF
Meyers – Blakely – C
Miles – Blakely – OF, P
Minchew – Dawson – P
Mitchell, Orion – Albany – OF, P
Mize – Blakely – C
Morgan – Arlington, Bainbridge – C
Morris – Blakely – OF, P
Mosely, Red – Bainbridge – P, MGR
Motts – Americus – P
Neil – Blakely – 2B
Nolan, Bill – Americus – 2B
Norris, Wally – Albany, Arlington, Americus – P
Overstreet, Morris – Americus, Dawson – P

Owens, Lefty – Americus – P
Pantone, Clifford M. "Cliff" – Americus – OF
Parker, Jasper "Jap" – Americus – OF
Parrish – Bainbridge – OF
Parsons, Bill "Big Bill" – Americus – OF, P
Paul – Americus – P, OF
Pinkston – Americus, Arlington – 2B
Pfeiffer – Dawson – P
Player, Edwin – Americus – OF
Poore, Shorty – Dawson, Blakely – OF
Pounds, Polly – Blakely – OF
Randolph (Pinkston) – Americus – 2B
Rawson, Clarence – Dawson – OF
Rawson, Eddie – Dawson – C
Reed, Milton D. – Albany – SS, MGR
Roberts, Yank – Bainbridge – P
Rose – Blakely – SS, 2B
Rosenfeld – Dawson, Bainbridge – OF
Sheppard – Albany - P
Sheppard – Bainbridge – OF
Slappey, John "Jack" – Albany – P
Smith (Dumas) – Americus – SS
Smith, Consuello – Arlington – OF, 3B
Spikes – Americus – OF
Stone, William Arthur "Tige" – Arlington – P, OF
Sullivan – Dawson – P, OF
Swann – Bainbridge – P
Swann, Duck – Albany – UT
Thrasher, George – Blakely – 2B
Thrasher, Ike – Arlington – 3B
Turk, Lucas Newton "Terrible" – Blakely – P
Wade, Eddie – Americus – OF
Wade, Wallace – Blakely – P, MGR
Wagoner – Blakely – SS
Walton – Americus – C, 1B
Walton – Bainbridge – OF
Watts – Bainbridge – P
Webb – Dawson, Bainbridge – 1B, 3B
Wheeler – Bainbridge – 3B
Wilder, Baby – Arlington, Bainbridge – P
Wilkes, Isben Giddens "Gid" – Americus, Blakely – 3B, SS
Williams, Bill – Americus – 3B
Williamson, Buddy – Blakely, Americus – P
Wingard, Ernest James, Sr. "Lefty" – Americus – P, OF
Winn – Dawson, Blakely – OF, C
Woodruff, Tobe – Blakely – 3B
Wright, Howard – Americus – C

Major League South Georgia Leaguers

Brannan, Otis Owen "George" – played for the St. Louis Browns in 1928 and 1929 for a total of 158 games.

Cochran, Alvah Jackson "Goat" – pitched for the Cincinnati Reds in 1915 for two innings in one game.

Elmore, Verdo Wilson, Sr. "Ellie" – played for the St. Louis Browns in 1924 for seven games.

Farmer, Floyd Haskell "Jack" – played for the Pittsburgh Pirates in 1916 for 55 games and for the Cleveland Indians in 1918 for seven games.

Jackson, Joseph Jefferson "Shoeless Joe" – played for the Philadelphia Athletics in 1908 and 1909, the Cleveland Indians from 1910 to 1915, and the Chicago White Sox from 1915 to 1920.

Koenigsmark, William Thomas "Will" – pitched in one game for the St. Louis Cardinals in 1919. He faced three batters, one getting a single, and the other two walking.

Kroh, Floyd Myron "Rube" – pitched for the Boston Red Sox in 1906 and 1907, the Chicago Cubs from 1908 through 1910, and the Boston Braves in 1912. His total record was 14 wins and 9 losses in 36 games pitched.

Marquardt, Albert Ludwig "Ollie" – played for the Boston Red Sox in 1931 for 17 games.

Reed, Milton D. – played for the St. Louis Cardinals for one game in 1911, the Philadelphia Phillies for 57 games between 1913 and 1914, and the Brooklyn Tip-Tops of the Federal League for 10 games in 1915.

Slappey, John "Jack" – pitched in three games for the Philadelphia Athletics in 1920.

Stone, William Arthur "Tige" – pitched three innings in one game for the St. Louis Cardinals at the end of the 1923 season.

Turk, Lucas Newton "Terrible" – pitched in five games for the Washington Senators in 1922.

Wingard, Ernest James, Sr. "Lefty" – pitched for the St. Louis Browns in 145 games from 1924 through 1927. His major league pitching record was 29 wins and 43 losses.

1923 Americus Daily Lineups

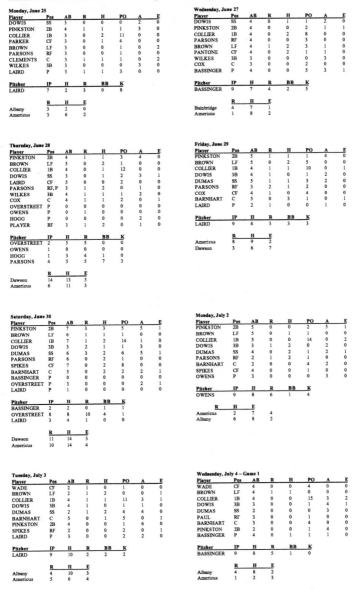

Monday, June 25

Player	Pos	AB	R	H	PO	A	E
DOWIS	SS	3	0	0	0	2	0
PINKSTON	2B	4	1	1	1	3	0
COLLIER	1B	3	0	2	11	0	0
PARKER	CF	3	0	1	4	0	0
BROWN	LF	3	0	0	1	0	2
PARSONS	RF	3	0	0	1	0	0
CLEMENTS	C	3	1	1	1	0	2
WILKES	3B	3	0	0	0	3	0
LAIRD	P	3	1	1	3	0	0

Pitcher	IP	H	R	BB	K
LAIRD	7	2	3	0	8

	R	H	E
Albany	3	2	0
Americus	3	6	2

Wednesday, June 27

Player	Pos	AB	R	H	PO	A	E
DOWIS	SS	4	0	1	1	2	0
PINKSTON	2B	4	0	0	2	1	1
COLLIER	1B	4	0	2	8	0	0
PARSONS	RF	4	0	0	3	0	0
BROWN	LF	4	1	2	3	1	0
PANTONE	CF	4	0	2	1	1	0
WILKES	3B	3	0	0	0	3	0
COX	C	3	0	0	2	0	0
BASSINGER	P	4	0	0	5	3	1

Pitcher	IP	H	R	BB	K
BASSINGER	9	7	4	2	5

	R	H	E
Bainbridge	4	7	1
Americus	1	8	2

Thursday, June 28

Player	Pos	AB	R	H	PO	A	E
PINKSTON	2B	4	1	1	3	4	0
BROWN	LF	5	0	2	1	0	0
COLLIER	1B	4	0	1	12	0	0
DOWIS	SS	3	0	1	2	3	1
LAIRD	CF	5	0	0	2	0	0
PARSONS	RF, P	3	1	2	0	1	0
WILKES	3B	4	1	1	1	2	0
COX	C	4	1	1	2	0	1
OVERSTREET	P	0	0	0	0	0	0
OWENS	P	0	1	0	0	0	0
HOGG	P	0	0	0	0	2	0
PLAYER	RF	3	1	2	0	1	0

Pitcher	IP	H	R	BB	K
OVERSTREET	2	5	5	0	0
OWENS	1	0	0	0	0
HOGG	1	3	4	1	0
PARSONS	4	5	5	7	3

	R	H	E
Dawson	14	13	5
Americus	6	11	3

Friday, June 29

Player	Pos	AB	R	H	PO	A	E
PINKSTON	2B	5	1	1	1	4	0
BROWN	LF	5	0	2	5	0	0
COLLIER	1B	4	1	1	10	0	1
DOWIS	3B	4	1	0	1	2	0
DUMAS	SS	5	1	1	3	2	0
PARSONS	RF	3	0	1	2	0	0
COX	CF	4	1	0	4	0	0
BARNHART	C	5	0	3	1	0	1
LAIRD	P	2	1	0	0	1	0

Pitcher	IP	H	R	BB	K
LAIRD	9	6	3	3	3

	R	H	E
Americus	8	9	2
Dawson	3	6	7

Saturday, June 30

Player	Pos	AB	R	H	PO	A	E
PINKSTON	2B	7	3	3	5	5	1
BROWN	LF	6	1	1	1	0	0
COLLIER	1B	7	1	2	14	1	0
DOWIS	3B	3	2	1	1	3	0
DUMAS	SS	6	3	2	6	5	1
PARSONS	RF	6	0	2	1	0	0
SPIKES	CF	7	0	2	8	0	0
BARNHART	C	5	0	2	2	2	1
BASSINGER	P	0	0	0	0	0	0
OVERSTREET	P	3	0	0	0	2	1
LAIRD	P	1	0	0	0	0	0

Pitcher	IP	H	R	BB	K
BASSINGER	2	2	0	1	1
OVERSTREET	8	8	10	4	1
LAIRD	3	4	1	0	0

	R	H	E
Dawson	11	14	3
Americus	10	14	4

Monday, July 2

Player	Pos	AB	R	H	PO	A	E
PINKSTON	2B	5	0	0	2	5	1
BROWN	LF	5	0	1	1	0	0
COLLIER	1B	5	0	0	14	0	2
DOWIS	3B	3	1	2	0	2	0
DUMAS	SS	4	0	2	1	2	1
PARSONS	RF	2	1	2	1	0	0
BARNHART	C	2	0	0	4	2	0
SPIKES	CF	4	0	0	1	0	0
OWENS	P	3	0	0	0	3	0

Pitcher	IP	H	R	BB	K
OWENS	9	8	6	1	4

	R	H	E
Americus	2	7	4
Albany	6	8	2

Tuesday, July 3

Player	Pos	AB	R	H	PO	A	E
WADE	CF	2	1	0	1	0	0
BROWN	LF	3	1	2	0	0	1
COLLIER	1B	4	1	1	11	3	1
DOWIS	3B	4	0	1	1	1	0
DUMAS	SS	2	1	2	4	4	0
BARNHART	C	5	0	1	5	0	1
PINKSTON	2B	4	0	0	1	6	0
SPIKES	RF	2	0	0	2	0	1
LAIRD	P	3	0	0	2	2	0

Pitcher	IP	H	R	BB	K
LAIRD	9	10	2	2	2

	R	H	E
Albany	4	10	3
Americus	5	6	4

Wednesday, July 4 – Game 1

Player	Pos	AB	R	H	PO	A	E
WADE	CF	4	0	0	4	0	0
BROWN	LF	4	1	1	0	0	0
COLLIER	1B	4	0	0	15	3	2
DOWIS	3B	3	0	0	1	4	1
DUMAS	SS	2	0	0	0	3	0
PAUL	RF	3	0	0	1	0	0
BARNHART	C	3	0	0	4	0	0
PINKSTON	2B	2	0	0	1	4	0
BASSINGER	P	4	0	1	1	1	0

Pitcher	IP	H	R	BB	K
BASSINGER	9	8	5	1	0

	R	H	E
Albany	4	8	2
Americus	1	2	3

Wednesday, July 4 – Game 2

Player	Pos	AB	R	H	PO	A	E
WADE	CF	5	2	2	4	0	0
BROWN	LF	5	1	1	0	0	0
COLLIER	1B	4	1	1	10	1	1
DOWIS	2B	3	1	1	2	1	0
DUMAS	SS	4	0	1	2	1	0
PARSONS	RF	5	0	0	1	0	0
PAUL	P	4	0	0	0	3	0
BARNHART	C	4	0	2	4	1	0
PINKSTON	2B	4	0	0	3	2	0

Pitcher	IP	H	R	BB	K
PAUL	9	9	8	4	4

	R	H	E
Americus	5	8	1
Albany	8	9	3

Thursday, July 5

Player	Pos	AB	R	H	PO	A	E
WADE	CF	3	0	1	5	0	2
PINKSTON	2B	4	0	0	4	3	1
COLLIER	1B	4	1	1	2	6	0
DOWIS	3B	3	0	1	1	0	1
DUMAS	SS	4	1	0	2	2	1
PARSONS	LF	3	1	1	4	0	0
PAUL	RF	2	0	0	2	0	1
BARNHART	CF	2	0	2	3	1	0
OWENS	P	2	0	0	0	0	0

Pitcher	IP	H	R	BB	K
OWENS	9	5	2	0	2

	R	H	E
Blakely	2	5	0
Americus	3	7	6

Friday, July 6

Player	Pos	AB	R	H	PO	A	E
WADE	CF	5	0	0	4	0	0
COLLIER	1B	4	1	1	15	0	0
WILKES	3B	5	1	0	3	2	1
DUMAS	SS	4	1	2	1	2	0
BARNHART	C	3	2	2	5	1	0
PAUL	RF	5	0	1	0	0	0
BROWN	LF	5	0	1	0	0	0
PINKSTON	2B	2	0	0	2	6	0
LAIRD	P	4	0	0	0	4	0

Pitcher	IP	H	R	BB	K
LAIRD	9	7	3	3	6

	R	H	E
Blakely	3	7	2
Americus	4	9	1

Saturday, July 7

Player	Pos	AB	R	H	PO	A	E
WADE	CF	4	1	2	1	0	0
COLLIER	1B	4	1	2	13	0	0
WILKES	3B	3	2	1	1	3	0
DUMAS	SS	4	1	0	2	4	0
BARNHART	C	4	1	2	4	1	0
PAUL	RF	3	0	1	1	0	1
BROWN	LF	4	0	1	2	0	0
PINKSTON	2B	4	1	1	3	3	0
BASSINGER	P	4	0	0	0	1	0

Pitcher	IP	H	R	BB	K
BASSINGER	9	6	3	2	4

	R	H	E
Americus	7	9	1
Blakely	3	6	1

Monday, July 9

Player	Pos	AB	R	H	PO	A	E
WADE	CF	4	0	3	2	0	0
WILKES	3B	4	0	1	1	0	1
BARNHART	RF	3	0	0	0	0	0
DUMAS	SS	2	0	2	1	3	1
WRIGHT	C	3	0	0	4	0	0
BROWN	LF	3	0	0	0	0	0
COLLIER	1B	3	0	1	13	0	2
PINKSTON	2B	3	0	0	0	2	1
PAUL	P	3	0	1	0	8	0

Pitcher	IP	H	R	BB	K
PAUL	7	5	3	3	3

	R	H	E
Arlington	3	5	0
Americus	0	8	5

Tuesday, July 10

Player	Pos	AB	R	H	PO	A	E
WADE	CF	5	0	0	3	0	0
WILKES	3B	4	0	2	1	3	2
BARNHART	RF	4	0	1	0	0	0
DUMAS	SS	4	0	1	4	2	1
BROWN	LF	4	0	1	0	0	0
COLLIER	1B	4	0	0	11	1	1
WRIGHT	C	2	0	1	2	2	0
PINKSTON	2B	4	0	1	6	5	0
OWENS	P	3	0	0	0	4	0

Pitcher	IP	H	R	BB	K
OWENS	9	10	7	2	2

	R	H	E
Arlington	7	10	1
Americus	0	7	4

Wednesday, July 11

Player	Pos	AB	R	H	PO	A	E
WILKES	3B	5	0	0	0	3	0
PINKSTON	2B	5	0	1	3	5	0
BARNHART	C	5	1	1	2	1	0
WADE	CF	3	1	1	2	0	0
DUMAS	SS	4	1	3	1	2	0
PAUL	RF	4	2	2	1	0	0
BROWN	LF	2	0	0	1	0	0
COLLIER	1B	4	0	3	14	0	0
LAIRD	P	3	0	0	0	2	0

Pitcher	IP	H	R	BB	K
LAIRD	8	11	6	1	0

	R	H	E
Americus	5	10	0
Arlington	6	11	2

Thursday, July 12

Player	Pos	AB	R	H	PO	A	E
WILKES	3B	4	1	1	1	2	0
PINKSTON	2B	4	0	0	4	2	0
BARNHART	C	4	1	2	2	2	0
WADE	CF	4	0	1	6	0	1
DUMAS	SS	4	1	2	3	2	2
PAUL	RF	4	0	0	0	0	1
COLLIER	1B	4	1	2	8	0	1
BROWN	LF	4	0	0	0	0	1
BASSINGER	P	4	1	0	0	0	0

Pitcher	IP	H	R	BB	K
BASSINGER	9	11	8	0	3

	R	H	E
Americus	5	8	6
Arlington	8	11	5

Friday, July 13

Player	Pos	AB	R	H	PO	A	E
WILKES	3B	4	1	1	0	0	1
PINKSTON	2B	5	1	1	2	0	0
BARNHART	C	5	1	1	6	0	0
WADE	CF	5	0	1	2	1	1
DUMAS	SS	5	3	4	2	3	1
PAUL	LF, P	5	2	2	1	1	1
COLLIER	1B	4	0	2	12	0	1
LAIRD	P, LF	4	1	0	1	0	0
BROWN	RF	4	0	1	1	0	0

Pitcher	IP	H	R	BB	K
LAIRD	4	2	3	2	2
PAUL	6	2	2	2	2

	R	H	E
Americus	9	13	5
Blakely	5	4	3

Saturday, July 14 – Game 1

Player	Pos	AB	R	H	PO	A	E
WILKES	3B	3	0	0	1	1	0
PINKSTON	2B	2	1	0	1	4	0
BARNHART	C	3	2	1	3	0	0
WADE	CF	2	3	1	5	0	0
DUMAS	SS	4	3	2	2	2	2
PAUL	LF	4	2	2	2	0	0
COLLIER	1B	4	1	2	7	0	0
PARSONS	RF	3	0	1	0	0	0
LAIRD	P	3	0	0	0	2	0

Pitcher	IP	H	R	BB	K
LAIRD	9	3	1	1	2

	R	H	E
Blakely	1	3	3
Americus	12	9	2

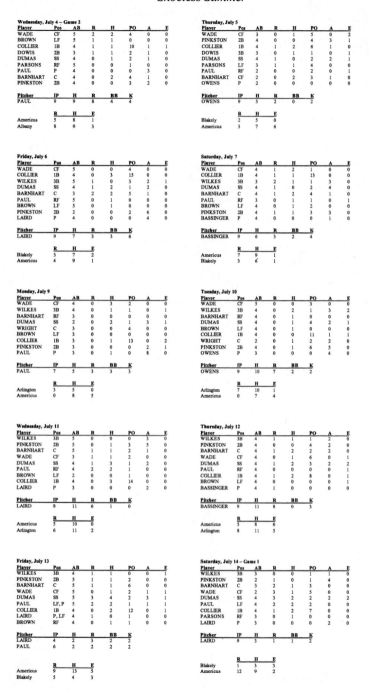

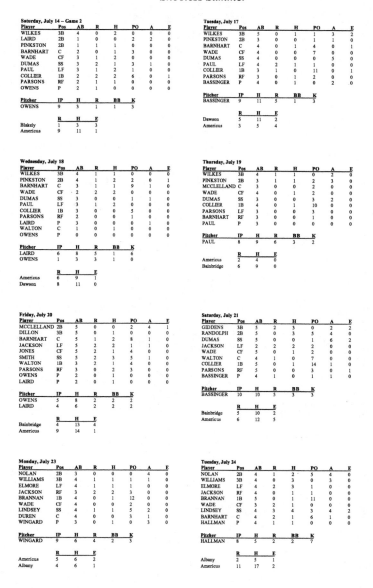

Saturday, July 14 – Game 2

Player	Pos	AB	R	H	PO	A	E
WILKES	3B	4	0	2	0	0	0
LAIRD	2B	1	0	0	2	2	0
PINKSTON	2B	1	1	1	0	0	0
BARNHART	C	2	0	1	3	0	0
WADE	CF	3	1	2	0	0	0
DUMAS	SS	3	2	1	3	1	0
PAUL	LF	3	1	2	1	0	0
COLLIER	1B	2	2	2	6	0	1
PARSONS	RF	2	1	1	0	0	0
OWENS	P	2	1	0	0	0	0

Pitcher	IP	H	R	BB	K
OWENS	9	3	1	1	3

	R	H	E
Blakely	1	3	3
Americus	9	11	1

Wednesday, July 18

Player	Pos	AB	R	H	PO	A	E
WILKES	3B	4	1	1	0	0	0
PINKSTON	2B	4	1	2	2	0	1
BARNHART	C	3	1	1	9	1	0
WADE	CF	2	2	2	0	0	0
DUMAS	SS	3	0	0	1	1	0
PAUL	LF	3	1	2	0	0	0
COLLIER	1B	3	0	0	5	0	0
PARSONS	RF	2	0	0	1	0	0
LAIRD	P	3	0	0	0	1	0
WALTON	C	1	0	1	0	0	0
OWENS	P	0	0	0	0	0	0

Pitcher	IP	H	R	BB	K
LAIRD	6	8	5	1	6
OWENS	1	3	3	1	0

	R	H	E
Americus	6	9	1
Dawson	8	11	0

Friday, July 20

Player	Pos	AB	R	H	PO	A	E
MCCLELLAND	2B	5	0	0	2	4	1
DILLON	3B	5	0	1	0	0	0
BARNHART	C	5	1	2	8	1	0
JACKSON	LF	5	2	2	1	1	0
JONES	CF	5	2	1	4	0	0
SMITH	SS	5	2	3	5	1	0
WALTON	1B	3	2	1	4	0	0
PARSONS	RF	3	0	2	3	0	0
OWENS	P	2	0	1	0	0	0
LAIRD	P	2	0	1	0	0	0

Pitcher	IP	H	R	BB	K
OWENS	5	8	2	2	2
LAIRD	4	6	2	2	2

	R	H	E
Bainbridge	4	13	4
Americus	9	14	1

Monday, July 23

Player	Pos	AB	R	H	PO	A	E
NOLAN	2B	3	0	0	0	4	0
WILLIAMS	3B	4	1	1	1	1	0
ELMORE	LF	4	1	1	1	0	0
JACKSON	RF	3	2	2	3	0	0
BRANNAN	1B	4	0	1	12	0	0
WADE	CF	4	0	0	2	0	0
LINDSEY	SS	4	1	1	5	2	0
DUREN	C	4	0	0	3	1	0
WINGARD	P	3	0	1	0	3	0

Pitcher	IP	H	R	BB	K
WINGARD	9	6	4	2	3

	R	H	E
Americus	5	6	2
Albany	4	6	1

Tuesday, July 17

Player	Pos	AB	R	H	PO	A	E
WILKES	3B	5	0	1	1	3	2
PINKSTON	2B	3	0	0	1	1	0
BARNHART	C	4	0	1	4	0	1
WADE	CF	4	0	0	7	0	0
DUMAS	SS	4	0	0	0	5	0
PAUL	LF	4	2	1	1	0	0
COLLIER	1B	3	1	0	11	0	1
PARSONS	RF	3	0	1	2	0	0
BASSINGER	P	4	0	1	0	2	0

Pitcher	IP	H	R	BB	K
BASSINGER	9	11	5	1	3

	R	H	E
Dawson	5	11	2
Americus	3	5	4

Thursday, July 19

Player	Pos	AB	R	H	PO	A	E
WILKES	3B	4	1	1	0	2	0
PINKSTON	2B	4	0	1	2	3	0
MCCLELLAND	C	3	0	0	2	0	0
WADE	CF	4	0	1	2	0	0
DUMAS	SS	3	0	0	3	2	0
COLLIER	1B	4	0	1	10	0	0
PARSONS	LF	3	0	0	3	0	0
BARNHART	RF	3	0	0	1	0	0
PAUL	P	3	0	0	0	0	0

Pitcher	IP	H	R	BB	K
PAUL	8	9	6	3	2

	R	H	E
Americus	2	4	0
Bainbridge	6	9	0

Saturday, July 21

Player	Pos	AB	R	H	PO	A	E
GIDDENS	3B	5	2	3	0	2	2
RANDOLPH	2B	5	0	3	5	4	0
DUMAS	SS	5	0	0	1	6	2
JACKSON	LF	5	2	2	2	0	0
WADE	CF	5	0	1	2	0	0
WALTON	C	4	1	0	7	0	0
COLLIER	1B	5	0	1	14	1	0
PARSONS	RF	5	0	0	3	0	1
BASSINGER	P	4	1	0	1	1	0

Pitcher	IP	H	R	BB	K
BASSINGER	10	10	5	3	3

	R	H	E
Bainbridge	5	10	2
Americus	6	12	5

Tuesday, July 24

Player	Pos	AB	R	H	PO	A	E
NOLAN	2B	4	1	2	5	4	0
WILLIAMS	3B	4	0	3	0	3	0
ELMORE	LF	4	2	3	1	0	0
JACKSON	RF	4	0	1	1	0	0
BRANNAN	1B	5	0	1	11	0	0
WADE	CF	3	2	1	0	0	0
LINDSEY	SS	4	3	4	3	4	2
BARNHART	C	4	2	1	6	1	0
HALLMAN	P	4	1	1	0	0	0

Pitcher	IP	H	R	BB	K
HALLMAN	8	5	2	2	7

	R	H	E
Albany	2	5	1
Americus	11	17	2

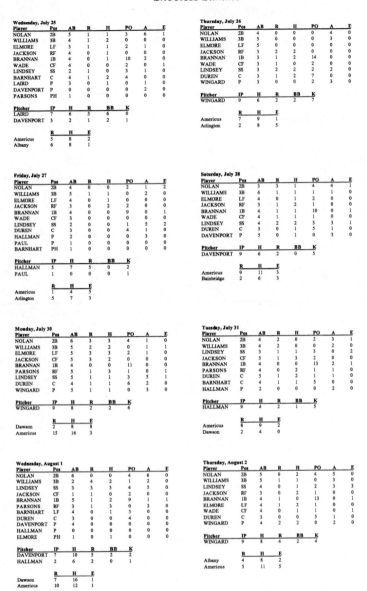

Wednesday, July 25

Player	Pos	AB	R	H	PO	A	E
NOLAN	2B	5	1	1	3	6	1
WILLIAMS	3B	4	1	2	0	0	0
ELMORE	LF	3	1	1	2	1	0
JACKSON	RF	4	0	1	0	0	0
BRANNAN	1B	4	0	1	10	2	0
WADE	CF	4	0	0	2	0	1
LINDSEY	SS	2	1	0	3	1	0
BARNHART	C	4	1	2	4	0	0
LAIRD	P	3	0	1	0	1	0
DAVENPORT	P	0	0	0	0	2	0
PARSONS	PH	1	0	0	0	0	0

Pitcher	IP	H	R	BB	K
LAIRD	7	6	5	6	0
DAVENPORT	3	2	1	2	1

	R	H	E
Americus	5	8	2
Albany	6	8	1

Thursday, July 26

Player	Pos	AB	R	H	PO	A	E
NOLAN	2B	4	0	0	0	4	0
WILLIAMS	3B	5	0	0	0	3	0
ELMORE	LF	5	0	0	0	0	0
JACKSON	RF	3	2	2	0	0	0
BRANNAN	1B	3	1	2	14	0	0
WADE	CF	3	1	0	2	0	0
LINDSEY	SS	3	2	2	2	2	0
DUREN	C	3	1	2	7	0	0
WINGARD	P	3	0	0	2	3	0

Pitcher	IP	H	R	BB	K
WINGARD	9	6	2	2	7

	R	H	E
Americus	7	9	1
Arlington	2	8	5

Friday, July 27

Player	Pos	AB	R	H	PO	A	E
NOLAN	2B	4	0	0	2	1	2
WILLIAMS	3B	5	1	1	0	2	0
ELMORE	LF	4	0	1	0	0	0
JACKSON	RF	3	0	2	2	0	0
BRANNAN	1B	4	0	1	9	0	1
WADE	CF	3	0	0	0	0	0
LINDSEY	SS	2	0	0	1	5	2
DUREN	C	3	0	0	4	1	0
HALLMAN	P	2	0	0	0	3	0
PAUL	P	1	0	0	0	0	0
BARNHART	PH	1	0	0	0	0	0

Pitcher	IP	H	R	BB	K
HALLMAN	5	7	5	0	2
PAUL	1	0	0	0	1

	R	H	E
Americus	1	4	5
Arlington	5	7	3

Saturday, July 28

Player	Pos	AB	R	H	PO	A	E
NOLAN	2B	3	3	1	4	4	1
WILLIAMS	3B	6	1	1	1	1	0
ELMORE	LF	4	0	1	2	0	0
JACKSON	RF	3	1	2	1	0	0
BRANNAN	1B	4	1	1	10	0	1
WADE	CF	4	1	1	1	0	0
LINDSEY	SS	4	2	2	3	3	1
DAVENPORT	P	5	0	1	0	3	0

Pitcher	IP	H	R	BB	K
DAVENPORT	9	6	2	0	5

	R	H	E
Americus	9	11	3
Bainbridge	2	6	3

Monday, July 30

Player	Pos	AB	R	H	PO	A	E
NOLAN	2B	6	3	3	4	1	0
WILLIAMS	3B	5	2	2	0	1	1
ELMORE	LF	5	3	3	2	1	0
JACKSON	CF	5	3	2	0	0	0
BRANNAN	1B	4	0	0	11	0	0
PARSONS	RF	5	1	3	1	0	1
LINDSEY	SS	5	1	1	3	5	1
DUREN	C	4	1	1	6	2	0
WINGARD	P	5	1	1	0	3	0

Pitcher	IP	H	R	BB	K
WINGARD	9	8	2	2	6

	R	H	E
Dawson	2	8	8
Americus	15	16	3

Tuesday, July 31

Player	Pos	AB	R	H	PO	A	E
NOLAN	2B	4	2	0	2	3	1
WILLIAMS	3B	4	2	0	0	2	0
LINDSEY	SS	3	1	1	3	0	2
JACKSON	CF	5	1	3	2	0	0
BRANNAN	1B	4	0	0	13	2	1
PARSONS	RF	4	0	2	1	1	0
DUREN	C	5	1	2	1	1	0
BARNHART	C	4	1	1	5	0	0
HALLMAN	P	2	0	0	0	2	0

Pitcher	IP	H	R	BB	K
HALLMAN	9	4	2	1	5

	R	H	E
Americus	8	9	2
Dawson	2	4	0

Wednesday, August 1

Player	Pos	AB	R	H	PO	A	E
NOLAN	2B	6	0	0	4	6	0
WILLIAMS	3B	2	4	2	1	2	0
LINDSEY	SS	3	3	3	4	5	0
JACKSON	CF	1	1	0	2	0	0
BRANNAN	1B	5	1	2	9	1	1
PARSONS	RF	3	1	3	0	2	0
BARNHART	LF	4	0	1	3	0	0
DUREN	C	3	0	0	4	0	0
DAVENPORT	P	4	0	0	0	0	0
HALLMAN	P	0	0	0	0	0	0
ELMORE	PH	1	0	1	0	0	0

Pitcher	IP	H	R	BB	K
DAVENPORT	7	10	5	2	2
HALLMAN	2	6	2	0	1

	R	H	E
Dawson	7	16	1
Americus	10	12	1

Thursday, August 2

Player	Pos	AB	R	H	PO	A	E
NOLAN	2B	5	0	2	4	5	0
WILLIAMS	3B	5	1	1	0	3	0
LINDSEY	SS	4	0	1	2	3	3
JACKSON	RF	3	0	2	1	0	0
BRANNAN	1B	4	1	0	13	0	1
ELMORE	LF	4	1	2	1	0	0
WADE	CF	4	0	1	1	0	1
DUREN	C	3	0	0	5	1	0
WINGARD	P	4	2	2	0	2	0

Pitcher	IP	H	R	BB	K
WINGARD	9	8	4	2	4

	R	H	E
Albany	4	8	2
Americus	5	11	5

Friday, August 3

Player	Pos	AB	R	H	PO	A	E
NOLAN	2B	6	0	1	5	7	0
WILLIAMS	3B	4	0	1	3	0	0
LINDSEY	SS	5	0	0	3	0	0
JACKSON	RF	4	0	0	1	1	0
BRANNAN	1B	5	0	1	10	1	1
ELMORE	LF	4	1	2	2	0	0
WADE	CF	4	0	1	0	0	0
DUREN	C	5	1	1	9	2	0
HALLMAN	P	3	0	0	0	2	0

Pitcher	IP	H	R	BB	K
HALLMAN	11	11	3	2	3

	R	H	E
Albany	3	11	4
Americus	2	7	1

Saturday, August 4

Player	Pos	AB	R	H	PO	A	E
NOLAN	2B	4	0	1	3	6	1
WILLIAMS	3B	5	3	3	1	2	1
ELMORE	LF	3	0	0	1	1	0
JACKSON	CF	4	1	3	2	0	0
PARSONS	RF	3	0	1	0	0	0
BRANNAN	1B	2	0	0	8	1	1
BURROUGHS	1B	1	0	0	7	0	0
LINDSEY	SS	4	0	0	3	4	0
DUREN	C	3	0	0	3	0	0
DAVENPORT	P	4	0	0	0	6	0

Pitcher	IP	H	R	BB	K
DAVENPORT	9	8	2	1	1

	R	H	E
Americus	4	7	3
Albany	2	8	1

Monday, August 6

Player	Pos	AB	R	H	PO	A	E
NOLAN	2B	4	1	0	2	1	0
WILLIAMS	3B	4	2	3	1	5	3
ELMORE	LF	4	0	0	0	0	0
JACKSON	RF	5	1	3	1	0	0
BRANNAN	1B	5	1	0	10	1	0
WADE	CF	4	0	0	1	0	0
LINDSEY	SS	4	1	1	4	1	0
DUREN	C	3	0	0	4	1	0
WINGARD	P	3	0	0	1	3	0
DAVENPORT	P	0	0	0	0	0	0
LAIRD	P	0	0	0	0	0	0
BURROUGHS	PH	1	0	0	0	0	0
BARNHART	PH	1	0	0	0	0	0

Pitcher	IP	H	R	BB	K
WINGARD	5	14	11	0	0
DAVENPORT	1	1	2	0	0
LAIRD	2	4	2	0	0

	R	H	E
Americus	6	7	3
Arlington	15	19	5

Tuesday, August 7

Player	Pos	AB	R	H	PO	A	E
NOLAN	2B	5	1	1	5	4	0
WILLIAMS	3B	4	0	0	0	1	0
ELMORE	LF	4	1	1	0	0	0
JACKSON	CF	4	1	3	2	0	0
BRANNAN	1B	3	1	2	8	1	0
PARSONS	RF	4	0	2	1	0	0
LINDSEY	SS	3	0	0	3	2	0
BARNHART	C	3	0	1	8	0	0
HALLMAN	P	4	0	0	0	0	0

Pitcher	IP	H	R	BB	K
HALLMAN	9	4	3	2	8

	R	H	E
Americus	4	10	0
Arlington	3	4	0

Wednesday, August 8

Player	Pos	AB	R	H	PO	A	E
NOLAN	2B	4	3	3	6	3	0
WILLIAMS	3B	4	3	1	0	1	0
ELMORE	LF	5	3	4	0	0	0
JACKSON	CF	4	1	2	1	0	0
BRANNAN	1B	4	0	1	9	2	0
PARSONS	RF	5	0	1	0	0	0
LINDSEY	SS	5	2	3	8	7	0
DUREN	C	3	0	2	8	0	0
DAVENPORT	P	4	1	1	0	0	0

Pitcher	IP	H	R	BB	K
DAVENPORT	9	7	0	1	7

	R	H	E
Arlington	0	7	3
Americus	13	18	0

Thursday, August 9

Player	Pos	AB	R	H	PO	A	E
NOLAN	2B	4	0	0	0	3	0
WILLIAMS	3B	4	0	1	0	0	1
LINDSEY	SS	4	0	0	3	4	2
JACKSON	LF	2	1	1	0	0	0
BRANNAN	1B	4	1	2	12	2	0
PARSONS	RF	3	0	0	2	0	0
WADE	CF	4	0	0	0	0	0
DUREN	C	4	0	2	11	1	0
WINGARD	P	4	1	1	2	5	0
BURROUGHS	PH	1	1	0	0	0	0

Pitcher	IP	H	R	BB	K
WINGARD	9	4	4	3	11

	R	H	E
Bainbridge	4	4	0
Americus	4	8	1

Friday, August 10

Player	Pos	AB	R	H	PO	A	E
NOLAN	2B	4	2	1	4	1	0
WILLIAMS	3B	4	0	3	1	3	0
LINDSEY	SS	5	1	2	2	5	1
JACKSON	CF	3	0	0	0	0	0
BRANNAN	1B	5	0	0	12	0	0
PARSONS	RF	4	0	2	1	0	0
WADE	LF	4	1	0	7	0	0
DUREN	C	2	0	0	0	1	0
MOTTS	P	3	1	1	0	0	0
BLOODWORTH	P	1	0	0	0	0	0

Pitcher	IP	H	R	BB	K
MOTTS	7	7	5	5	4
BLOODWORTH	2	2	0	0	2

	R	H	E
Americus	5	9	1
Bainbridge	5	9	1

Saturday, August 11

Player	Pos	AB	R	H	PO	A	E
WILLIAMS	3B	4	1	0	0	1	0
NOLAN	2B	4	1	2	3	2	0
BURROUGHS	LF	4	2	2	1	0	0
JACKSON	CF	5	1	1	0	0	0
BRANNAN	1B	4	0	1	6	0	1
PARSONS	RF	3	0	2	2	0	1
LINDSEY	SS	4	0	1	1	2	0
DUREN	C	4	0	0	11	0	0
HALLMAN	P	4	0	0	0	2	0

Pitcher	IP	H	R	BB	K
HALLMAN	9	3	0	1	11

	R	H	E
Americus	5	9	2
Bainbridge	0	3	2

117

Sunday, August 12 – Exhibition Game in Montgomery, Alabama

Player	Pos	AB	R	H	PO	A	E
NOLAN	2B	4	0	0	1	3	0
WILLIAMS	3B	3	1	0	1	5	0
ELMORE	LF	3	0	1	0	0	0
JACKSON	CF	3	1	1	1	0	0
BRANNAN	1B	3	0	0	17	2	0
PARSONS	RF	4	0	1	1	0	0
LINDSEY	SS	3	1	1	0	3	1
BARNHART	C	3	0	1	4	1	0
WINGARD	P	3	0	1	2	5	0

Pitcher	IP	H	R	BB	K
WINGARD	9	6	3	1	3

	R	H	E
Bainbridge	1	6	5
Americus	3	6	1

Monday, August 13

Player	Pos	AB	R	H	PO	A	E
NOLAN	2B	3	0	0	2	4	0
WILLIAMS	3B	3	0	1	0	0	1
ELMORE	LF	3	0	0	0	0	0
JACKSON	RF	3	1	1	0	0	0
FOLMAR	CF	2	1	0	1	0	0
BRANNAN	1B	2	0	2	8	1	1
LINDSEY	SS	2	1	0	0	2	0
DUREN	C	3	0	1	6	0	0
NORRIS	P	3	0	2	0	3	0

Pitcher	IP	H	R	BB	K
NORRIS	6	4	2	1	5

	R	H	E
Blakely	2	4	0
Americus	3	7	2

Tuesday, August 14

Player	Pos	AB	R	H	PO	A	E
NOLAN	2B	3	0	0	1	3	0
WILLIAMS	3B	2	0	0	0	0	1
BURROUGHS	3B	1	0	0	1	1	1
ELMORE	LF	4	1	2	6	0	0
JACKSON	RF	3	1	1	1	0	0
BRANNAN	1B	2	1	1	10	0	0
LINDSEY	SS	2	0	1	2	2	0
FOLMAR	CF	3	1	1	0	0	0
DUREN	C	3	0	1	6	2	0
BLOODWORTH	P	3	0	0	0	2	0

Pitcher	IP	H	R	BB	K
BLOODWORTH	8	6	1	0	7

	R	H	E
Blakely	1	6	0
Americus	4	7	2

Wednesday, August 15

Player	Pos	AB	R	H	PO	A	E
NOLAN	2B	1	0	0	2	1	0
BURROUGHS	3B	3	0	0	1	3	0
WILLIAMS	3B	5	1	3	1	1	0
ELMORE	LF	5	1	2	2	0	1
JACKSON	RF	2	1	1	0	0	0
BRANNAN	1B	5	2	1	8	1	1
FOLMAR	CF	5	2	2	3	0	0
LINDSEY	SS	4	1	1	3	3	0
DUREN	C	5	0	1	4	1	0
DAVENPORT	P	1	0	0	0	0	1
WINGARD	P	0	0	0	0	0	0
NORRIS	P	3	0	1	0	1	0
PARSONS	PH	1	0	0	0	0	0

Pitcher	IP	H	R	BB	K
DAVENPORT	2	8	6	0	2
WINGARD	1	0	0	0	0
JACKSON	1	0	0	1	0
NORRIS	5	7	3	3	2

	R	H	E
Americus	8	12	3
Blakely	9	15	6

Thursday, August 16 – Game 1

Player	Pos	AB	R	H	PO	A	E
NOLAN	2B	5	1	0	3	0	1
WILLIAMS	3B	5	1	1	1	0	0
ELMORE	LF	4	1	1	6	1	0
JACKSON	RF	4	1	1	3	0	0
BRANNAN	1B	4	2	1	3	0	0
FOLMAR	CF	2	1	1	2	0	0
LINDSEY	SS	5	1	3	2	0	0
BARNHART	C	4	1	1	7	0	0
HALLMAN	P	5	0	2	0	1	0

Pitcher	IP	H	R	BB	K
HALLMAN	9	8	0	1	8

	R	H	E
Americus	8	11	1
Bainbridge	1	8	4

Thursday, August 16 – Game 2

Player	Pos	AB	R	H	PO	A	E
NOLAN	2B	3	1	1	3	2	0
WILLIAMS	3B	3	1	1	6	1	0
ELMORE	LF	3	1	2	1	0	0
JACKSON	RF	3	1	2	1	0	0
BRANNAN	1B	2	1	0	8	0	0
FOLMAR	CF	3	1	1	0	0	0
LINDSEY	SS	3	0	1	0	1	0
DUREN	C	2	0	1	6	0	0
WINGARD	P	3	0	0	0	0	0

Pitcher	IP	H	R	BB	K
WINGARD	5	5	1	0	6

	R	H	E
Americus	7	8	0
Bainbridge	1	5	3

Monday, August 20 – Game 1 League Championship Series

Player	Pos	AB	R	H	PO	A	E
NOLAN	2B	4	0	1	2	1	0
WILLIAMS	3B	5	0	1	1	1	0
ELMORE	LF	4	1	2	2	0	0
JACKSON	RF	3	2	1	6	0	0
BRANNAN	1B	4	1	1	5	0	0
FOLMAR	CF	3	0	1	0	0	0
LINDSEY	SS	4	0	1	3	3	1
DUREN	C	4	1	3	7	0	0
HALLMAN	P	3	0	0	1	0	0

Pitcher	IP	H	R	BB	K
HALLMAN	9	5	1	2	7

	R	H	E
Albany	1	5	0
Americus	5	11	1

Tuesday, August 21 – Game 2 League Championship Series

Player	Pos	AB	R	H	PO	A	E
NOLAN	2B	6	1	1	5	3	0
WILLIAMS	3B	6	4	3	1	1	1
ELMORE	LF	6	2	5	2	0	0
JACKSON	RF	6	2	3	1	0	0
BRANNAN	1B	6	1	2	9	0	0
FOLMAR	CF	5	3	1	3	0	0
LINDSEY	SS	4	3	2	1	1	0
DUREN	C	4	0	1	5	0	0
WINGARD	P	5	3	4	0	4	0
PARSONS	LF	0	0	0	0	0	0

Pitcher	IP	H	R	BB	K
WINGARD	9	4	4	2	5

	R	H	E
Americus	19	22	1
Albany	4	4	5

Wednesday, August 22 – Game 3 League Championship Series

Player	Pos	AB	R	H	PO	A	E
NOLAN	2B	5	1	3	3	3	1
WILLIAMS	3B	3	0	1	2	0	1
ELMORE	LF	3	0	1	1	0	0
JACKSON	RF	4	1	2	0	0	0
BRANNAN	1B	4	0	0	9	1	0
FOLMAR	CF	4	0	0	2	0	0
LINDSEY	SS	4	1	1	5	5	5
DUREN	C	3	0	1	3	0	0
BARNHART	C	1	0	1	2	0	0
WILLIAMSON	P	1	0	0	0	1	1
DAVENPORT	P	3	1	1	0	1	0
PARSONS	PH	1	0	1	0	0	0
BURROUGHS	PH	1	0	1	0	0	0

Pitcher	IP	H	R	BB	K
WILLIAMSON	4	8	10	5	0
DAVENPORT	5	2	2	2	2

	R	H	E
Albany	12	10	0
Americus	4	13	8

Thursday, August 23 – Game 4 League Championship Series

Player	Pos	AB	R	H	PO	A	E
NOLAN	2B	3	0	0	1	3	0
WILLIAMS	3B	5	1	1	1	3	0
ELMORE	LF	5	2	4	3	0	0
JACKSON	RF	3	1	2	1	0	1
BRANNAN	1B	5	1	1	12	0	2
FOLMAR	CF	5	0	1	1	1	0
LINDSEY	SS	4	1	1	4	2	2
DUREN	C	3	0	0	8	1	0
NORRIS	P	2	1	1	0	0	1
WINGARD	P	2	0	1	0	1	1

Pitcher	IP	H	R	BB	K
NORRIS	2	5	3	1	2
WINGARD	6	3	0	0	4

	R	H	E
Americus	7	12	6
Albany	3	8	4

Monday, August 27 – Game 5 League Championship Series

Player	Pos	AB	R	H	PO	A	E
NOLAN	2B	4	0	1	1	1	0
WILLIAMS	3B	4	0	0	0	0	0
ELMORE	LF	4	0	0	2	0	0
JACKSON	CF	4	0	2	5	0	0
BRANNAN	1B	4	0	0	11	0	0
PARSONS	RF	3	0	0	2	0	0
LINDSEY	SS	3	1	1	3	4	2
DUREN	C	3	0	3	3	2	0
HALLMAN	P	3	0	2	0	2	0

Pitcher	IP	H	R	BB	K
HALLMAN	9	8	5	1	1

	R	H	E
Albany	5	8	0
Americus	1	9	2

Tuesday, August 28 – Game 6 League Championship Series

Player	Pos	AB	R	H	PO	A	E
NOLAN	2B	5	0	1	3	5	0
WILLIAMS	3B	4	1	1	2	1	0
ELMORE	LF	4	0	0	0	0	0
JACKSON	CF	2	2	1	3	0	0
PARSONS	RF	4	1	1	1	0	0
BRANNAN	1B	4	1	2	9	0	1
LINDSEY	SS	2	0	1	3	1	1
DUREN	C	3	0	0	6	0	0
DAVENPORT	P	4	0	0	0	3	0
WINGARD	CF	0	0	0	0	1	0

Pitcher	IP	H	R	BB	K
DAVENPORT	9	13	0	1	3

	R	H	E
Americus	5	8	2
Albany	0	13	2

Bibliography

Albany Herald, Albany, Georgia, June 19, 1923 through August 29, 1923.

Americus Times-Recorder, Americus, Georgia, June 1, 1923 through August 29, 1923.

Atlanta Journal Constitution, Atlanta, Georgia, June 26, 1923 through August 29, 1923.

http://sportsillustraded.cnn.com/baseball/mlb/all_time_stats, website.

http://www.blackbetsy.com, website.

The Professional Baseball Player Database, Old-Time Date, Inc.: Shawnee Mission. Version 4.00.

Photographs and Graphics

Americus Times-Recorder advertisement graphics from June 22, 1923 courtesy of the Americus Times-Recorder.
Americus Times-Recorder advertisement graphics from June 23, 1923 courtesy of the Americus Times-Recorder.
Americus Times-Recorder advertisement graphics from July 5, 1923 courtesy of the Americus Times-Recorder.
Americus Times-Recorder advertisement graphics from July 19, 1923 courtesy of the Americus Times-Recorder.
Joe Jackson photograph from the July 20, 1923 edition of the Americus Times-Recorder courtesy of the Americus Times-Recorder.
Americus Times-Recorder advertisement graphics from July 20, 1923 courtesy of the Americus Times-Recorder.
Americus Times-Recorder advertisement graphics from July 23, 1923 courtesy of the Americus Times-Recorder.
Americus Times-Recorder advertisement graphics from August 1, 1923 courtesy of the Americus Times-Recorder.
Americus Times-Recorder advertisement graphics from August 2, 1923 courtesy of the Americus Times-Recorder.
Americus Times-Recorder advertisement graphics from August 13,

1923 courtesy of the Americus Times-Recorder.

Americus Times-Recorder advertisement graphics from August 16, 1923 courtesy of the Americus Times-Recorder.

Americus Times-Recorder advertisement graphics from August 21, 1923 courtesy of the Americus Times-Recorder.

Americus Team photograph from the Verdo Elmore, Jr. collection.

Barnhart photograph from the Verdo Elmore, Jr. collection.

Bassinger photograph from the Rotunda Yearbook, Southern Methodist, University, Dallas, Texas.

Bell photograph from the Americus Times-Recorder.

Bloodworth photograph from the Special Collections, Mercer University, Tarver Library, Macon, Georgia.

Brannan photograph from the Verdo Elmore, Jr. collection.

Burroughs photograph from the Verdo Elmore, Jr. collection.

Clements photograph from the Special Collections, Mercer University, Tarver Library, Macon, Georgia.

Collier photograph from Yamacraw Yearbook, Oglethorpe University, Atlanta, Georgia.

Cox photograph from the 1923 Entrenous, Samford University, Birmingham, Alabama.

Davenport photograph from the Verdo Elmore, Jr. collection.

Dowis photograph from the Special Collections, Mercer University, Tarver Library, Macon, Georgia.

Duren photograph from the Verdo Elmore, Jr. collection.

Elmore photograph from the Verdo Elmore, Jr. collection.

Hallman photograph from the Verdo Elmore, Jr. collection.

Jackson photograph from the Verdo Elmore, Jr. collection.

Laird photograph from the Davidson College Archives, Davidson College, Davidson, North Carolina.

Lindsey photograph from the Verdo Elmore, Jr. collection.

Nolan photograph from the Verdo Elmore, Jr. collection.

Parker photograph from the 1923 Americus High School yearbook, Americus, Georgia.

Parsons photograph from the Verdo Elmore, Jr. collection.

Player photograph from the 1923 Americus High School yearbook, Americus, Georgia.

Wade photograph from the Verdo Elmore, Jr. collection.

Wilkes photograph from Special Collections, Mercer University, Tarver Library, Macon, Georgia.

Williams photograph from the Verdo Elmore, Jr. collection.

Wingard photograph from the Verdo Elmore, Jr. collection.

Special Thanks to:

Harriett Bates and Helen Wishum at the Lake Blackshear Regional
   Library
Marie and Alf Bell
Mary Braswell at The Albany Herald
Susan Broome at Mercer University
Marion Clark
Cathy Dunnahoo
Dustin Edge at Davidson College
Verdo Elmore, Jr.
Richard Lytle and Michelle Gonzalez at Southern Methodist University
George Stewart at Oglethorpe University
Jennifer Taylor at Samford University
Janice Williams at the Dougherty County Public Library

A very special thanks to my wife, Virginia, for her support and patience
during the writing of this book and all the rest of the time she has
known me.

Most of all, I thank God for the many blessings He has given me.

William C. Webb

Mr. William Webb and myself

During my research of Shoeless Joe Jackson playing Americus, by mere coincidence, I came across a gentleman living at the Magnolia Manor retirement home in Americus by the name of William C. Webb. Mr. Webb had the very distinct privilege of actually playing baseball with Shoeless Joe Jackson in Waycross, Georgia in 1925 for the city's Atlantic Coastline railroad team. He looked to be in very good shape when I met him, and it was a great pleasure to talk to him about Shoeless Joe, baseball, and life in general.

Born in 1903 in Adrian, Georgia, William Webb graduated from Adrian High School in 1922. He played baseball, football, and basketball at Sparks Junior College from 1922 through 1924. After Sparks, Mr. Webb went to Waycross and was hired by the railroad "to play baseball." Joe Jackson was the player/manager of the team and had been there since the end of the 1923 season, immediately following his Americus playing time.

Mr. Webb pitched for the railroad team with Jackson through the 1925 season. In 1926, he pitched for the Midville, Georgia semi-pro baseball team and stayed there through 1928. He calls these years the best of his career that lasted for fourteen years total. In 1927, he started fifteen games, winning twelve, losing two, and tying one. In 1929 while pitching for Thomaston, Georgia, Mr. Webb pitched a game against Luke Appling's Grinnell team of East Atlanta and gave up only six hits. One of those hits was a home run hit by Appling who would begin a twenty-year major league career with the White Sox the very next year. Thomaston won the game 7 to 3 behind Mr. Webb's pitching of the complete game. He also got two hits in the game to help his cause.

In 1931, while in the United States Navy, Mr. Webb pitched on the USS Wright team. That same year, when the New York Yankees broke spring camp, they played an exhibition game against the Wright team. Pop Branch was on the mound for the Navy team and pitched well enough against Ruth and Gehrig that the Yankees offered him a contract to pitch for them.

Mr. Webb described Shoeless Joe Jackson as a good baseball man. Even though he was not educated, he had the ability to make managerial decisions that almost always worked out well. He was a "player's manager," according to Mr. Webb, who led by example and had great respect for the players. Shoeless Joe's very presence was a boost to the players he managed bringing each of them to the top of their game. Jackson also had more ability in baseball than anyone he had ever seen, both offensively and defensively, driving the ball out of the park almost at will, making circus catches in the outfield, and throwing the ball over the stands behind home from center field. When payday came, Joe would ask Mr. Webb to help him cash his paychecks assisting with signing his name on them.

Shoeless Joe told Mr. Webb how his bat, the famous "Black Betsy," was made of second-grown hickory wood. Mr. Webb described it as having a big knob, small at the handle, and bent. "The bend in the bat was how he got his hands through the ball so fast," Mr. Webb explained. Mr. Webb described the strange sound the bat made when it hit the ball as sounding "like he hit a brick." Jackson even let Mr. Webb hit with the bat a few times during the Waycross days.

At 98 years young, William Webb is one of the few people still around who saw Shoeless Joe Jackson play, much less played on the same team. He also saw and played with many of the great ball players of the 1920's and 30's. An afternoon talking with Mr. William Webb is truly both and honor and a pleasure.

About the Author

John Bell was born in Americus, Georgia in 1969 and lived there until 1995. He graduated from Americus High School in 1987 and earned a B.S. in Political Science with a minor in History from Georgia Southwestern State University in Americus in 1993.

Now living in Carrollton, Georgia, John is married to Virginia Williams Bell, and they have one son, Jacob.